Cambridge Elements

Elements in Global Philosophy of Religion
edited by
Yujin Nagasawa
University of Oklahoma

RELIGIOUS NATURALISM

John Bishop
University of Auckland

Ken Perszyk
The University of Waikato

Shaftesbury Road, Cambridge CB2 8EA, United Kingdom

One Liberty Plaza, 20th Floor, New York, NY 10006, USA

477 Williamstown Road, Port Melbourne, VIC 3207, Australia

314–321, 3rd Floor, Plot 3, Splendor Forum, Jasola District Centre,
New Delhi – 110025, India

103 Penang Road, #05–06/07, Visioncrest Commercial, Singapore 238467

Cambridge University Press is part of Cambridge University Press & Assessment,
a department of the University of Cambridge.

We share the University's mission to contribute to society through the pursuit of
education, learning and research at the highest international levels of excellence.

www.cambridge.org
Information on this title: www.cambridge.org/9781009469135

DOI: 10.1017/9781009469104

© John Bishop and Ken Perszyk 2025

This work is in copyright. It is subject to statutory exceptions and to the provisions of relevant licensing agreements; with the exception of the Creative Commons version the link for which is provided below, no reproduction of any part of this work may take place without the written permission of Cambridge University Press.

An online version of this work is published at doi.org/10.1017/9781009469104 under a Creative Commons Open Access licence CC-BY-NC 4.0 which permits re-use, distribution and reproduction in any medium for non-commercial purposes providing appropriate credit to the original work is given and any changes made are indicated. To view a copy of this licence, visit
https://creativecommons.org/licenses/by-nc/4.0

All versions of this work may contain content reproduced under license from third parties. Permission to reproduce this third-party content must be obtained from these third-parties directly.

When citing this work, please include a reference to the DOI 10.1017/9781009469104

First published 2025

A catalogue record for this publication is available from the British Library

ISBN 978-1-009-46913-5 Hardback
ISBN 978-1-009-46909-8 Paperback
ISSN 2976-5749 (online)
ISSN 2976-5730 (print)

Cambridge University Press & Assessment has no responsibility for the persistence or accuracy of URLs for external or third-party internet websites referred to in this publication and does not guarantee that any content on such websites is, or will remain, accurate or appropriate.

For EU product safety concerns, contact us at Calle de José Abascal, 56, 1°, 28003 Madrid, Spain, or email eugpsr@cambridge.org

Religious Naturalism

Elements in Global Philosophy of Religion

DOI: 10.1017/9781009469104
First published online: August 2025

John Bishop
University of Auckland

Ken Perszyk
The University of Waikato

Author for correspondence: John Bishop, jc.bishop@auckland.ac.nz

Abstract: Is a religious naturalism possible? 'Scientific' naturalism accommodates only 'thin' religiousness. A more robust religious naturalism posits an ultimate reality that supports the ideals of eco-morality and the hope that human fulfilment may be achieved by following those ideals. Such an account may yet be 'expansively' naturalist in taking the natural world to be the only (concrete) reality, and in not going against, only beyond, well-confirmed science. For the core content of an expansive religious naturalism, this Element proposes the idea of an inherent integrative cosmic purpose. The authors reflect both on Indigenous worldviews and on theist traditions in pursuing this proposal. This title is also available as open access on Cambridge Core.

This Element also has a video abstract:
www.cambridge.org/EGPR_Bishop_abstract

Keywords: religious naturalism, scientific naturalism, cosmic purpose, Indigenous worldviews, environmental ethics

© John Bishop and Ken Perszyk 2025

ISBNs: 9781009469135 (HB), 9781009469098 (PB), 9781009469104 (OC)
ISSNs: 2976-5749 (online), 2976-5730 (print)

Contents

1 Introduction: 'Religion without the Supernatural'   1

2 Understanding the *Religiousness* of Religious Naturalism   4

3 Understanding the *Naturalism* of Religious Naturalism   11

4 Religious Naturalism and Cosmic Purposiveness   22

5 Resources for a Robust Religious Naturalism   35

6 Conclusion: Challenges for Religious Naturalists   50

    References   59

1 Introduction: 'Religion without the Supernatural'

Religious naturalism is a broad church. It may be described, roughly, as a religious attitude or worldview that focuses on the natural world, rather than on some 'other worldly' realm 'above' or 'beyond' the natural world – 'religion without the supernatural', if one wants a slogan. We get a good general sense of religious naturalism by appreciating the motivations that attract people to it. It is attractive for those who feel that the natural world has its own intrinsic worth, and who are dissatisfied with religious traditions which seem to them to locate what's ultimately worthwhile 'elsewhere'. A further motivation comes from the desire for a religious outlook compatible with understanding the world 'naturalistically', using the methods of scientific inquiry which have led to so many benefits and successes in explaining and predicting natural phenomena. Historically, there has been a tension between a scientific understanding of the world and traditional religious perspectives. Yet many have felt that religion is still needed to provide something missing from a purely scientific worldview. Religion concerns fundamental values, and it offers meaningful ways of living that sustain hope for human fulfilment, both individually and collectively. A religious naturalism, then – if such a thing is possible – offers the prospect of preserving the ideals of religion within a worldview that 'takes science seriously'.

But the idea persists that a religious naturalism is *not* possible. 'Religious naturalism' seems to be an oxymoron because religion requires something – the 'supernatural' – which could not be admitted by a purely naturalist view of the world. There isn't anything manifestly incoherent, however, in the idea of a religious perspective that doesn't invoke anything beyond or above the natural world. In particular, the natural world may *itself* be taken as the fit object of religious attitudes, such as awe, reverence, and gratitude, and so be described as 'sacred', or 'holy', or even as 'divine'. Furthermore, this nature-focused religious perspective may have beneficial implications for human ways of living. A religious stance that attributes 'sacredness' to nature itself (or to some key feature of it) may be expected to support human behaviour aimed at conservation of ecosystems, preservation of species, and sustainable use of natural resources. An environmental ethics that mandates helpful responses to the ecological crises humanity now faces may thus potentially be supported by a nature-focused religious naturalism.

Advocacy for religious naturalism is often motivated, then, by its potential practical benefits in contrast to what is often assumed to be the failure of inherited 'Western' religious traditions. Lynn White (1967) argued that the roots of our ecological crisis – looming sixty years ago, and rapidly catching up with us now – lie in our 'Western' tendency to separate humanity from nature and to regard nature purely as a resource. This attitude, White observed, seems supported by the Judaeo-Christian Genesis myths, since they relate that man, made in the image of God, is given dominion over all other species. But the Genesis myths also feature a 'stewardship' theme: humanity is called to tend and care for the creation. And White himself urged his fellow Christians to return to the spirituality of Saint Francis of Assisi which emphasizes humanity's kinship with the wider creation.[1]

Nevertheless, many continue to think, rightly or wrongly, that the Abrahamic religious traditions downplay the natural world's significance and worth. It is not just that those traditions seem to endorse human domination over nature; they also locate ultimate human destiny in eternal life with God. That claim is often interpreted as implying that human 'salvation' can be achieved only beyond the natural world, which is therefore itself ultimately dispensable. A religious naturalism that attributes religious worth to nature and locates religious concerns wholly within the natural world can thus seem to many not only to be a coherent possibility but an obvious improvement as a religious option for the twenty-first century.[2]

In this Element we'll defend the view that there *can* be religious naturalisms: there need be no contradiction in terms in such an idea. We think that religious naturalisms can present inspiring religious possibilities, and that the topic of religious naturalism should be a central one for global philosophy of religion. To defend these views, however, it is necessary to confront the tension involved in being authentically religious within the limits of a genuinely naturalist view of the world. Those who advocate a religious naturalism that takes nature to be the appropriate object of religious attitudes are fully aware of this tension. Though they think their stance is religious in a worthwhile sense, many religious naturalists avoid deploying concepts of God or gods, since they assume that God or gods are supernatural beings of the type naturalism rules out. However, alternative concepts of divinity – that is, concepts which don't understand God, gods, or the divine as literally real supernatural beings – may fit with a naturalist perspective, at least on some accounts of what naturalism can admit. And some religious naturalists do indeed deploy God-talk.[3]

---

[1] For a recent review of the debate to which White's article gave rise, see Andrew Spencer (2019). (Spencer argues that a balanced Christian theology requires human concern for the whole creation.) The idea of a Biblical origin for human treatment of nature 'as a commodity belonging to us' is found also in Aldo Leopold (1949). Leopold was hugely influential in the conservation movement and the development of environmental ethics.

[2] Contemporary thinkers who, in varying ways, endorse this kind of option include Donald Crosby (2002), Ursula Goodenough (2023), Loyal Rue (2011), and Jerome Stone (2017).

[3] For example, Gordon Kaufman (2001), Karl Peters (2002 and 2022), and Stuart Kauffman (2008).

To specify a defensible kind or kinds of religious naturalism, it is essential to investigate different understandings of the two key terms, and then to identify some reasonable meaning or meanings of 'religious' which are compatible with some reasonable account of what it means to be 'naturalist'. The inquiry isn't purely a semantic one: rather, we need to grasp what is at stake, both in being religious, and in being naturalist, if a form of religious naturalism is to count as a live religious option. We'll therefore be considering both religiousness and naturalist commitment from a normative point of view – that is, in the light of what commitments (with their associated ways of living) we may reasonably think are *good* for us to have.

A significant part of our discussion is therefore taken up with conceptual investigation of what it may mean to be religious, and of what counts as 'naturalism'. Some forms of religious naturalism, we will suggest, achieve coherence only at the cost of a relatively thin form of religiousness. More robustly religious naturalisms go beyond 'scientific' naturalism in holding that there is more to reality than could be disclosed by science. Yet they may still take science seriously and be 'naturalist' if 'the more' required by their religious content is understood as belonging to *the one natural world* and not to any distinct supernatural order. We'll describe this kind of naturalism as *one-world-ist* naturalism. We will propose that a robustly religious naturalism may be achieved by understanding the one natural world as having an inherent cosmic purpose which humans may grasp, at least to the extent of understanding its practical implications for human existence in the wider environment. And we'll suggest that a metaphysics we call 'euteleology' provides an effective understanding of how purpose could be inherent in the natural world.

In this Element, then, we aim to investigate both religiousness and naturalist commitment in order to locate in conceptual space (and specify some content for) a worthwhile form or forms of religious naturalism. We cannot survey the whole 'broad church' of religious naturalism, nor properly trace its historical roots.[4] We'll mention some main contemporary varieties of religious naturalism, but we won't attempt to summarize or discuss in detail the particular accounts and arguments of individual authors.[5] Instead, our approach to

---

[4] So far as we're aware, the earliest use of the term 'religious naturalism' was in Tayler Lewis (1846: 282). The term was frequently used in theological circles in the United States in the early 1940s. Homer Dubs (1943) begins with the line: 'Religious naturalism is today one of the outstanding American philosophies of religion' (258). It's interesting to note, then, that as Jerome Stone points out, 'there was a near complete hiatus in the use of the term ['religious naturalism', and major publications in it] between 1946 and 1987' (12). For more on the hiatus and the earlier roots of religious naturalism in the States, see Stone (2008: 11–14 and 139–42).

[5] For a historically wide-ranging study of religious naturalism, starting with George Santayana and Samuel Alexander, see, e.g., Stone (2008). For detailed surveys of key contemporary figures, see, e.g., Michael Hogue (2010) and Mikael Leidenhag (2021).

understanding the 'territory' will be to undertake a structured discussion about how worthwhile religious naturalisms may be possible. Our interest here is in understanding *the content* of religious naturalist worldviews, not in trying to prove that any of them are true or likely to be true – though if a religious naturalism is to be a live option for contemporary faith it will be necessary that its stance on reality is at least possibly true.

We hope that our discussion provides a useful introduction for those yet to explore this field, as well as an aid to further understanding for those already familiar with it. Our discussion will, of course, be influenced by the contingent limitations of our backgrounds, and no doubt we won't always be sufficiently aware of the subtle forms that influence may take. It's therefore helpful for the reader to note that we are both from a 'Western' intellectual background. We are anglophone philosophers in the analytic tradition. Christianity (or perhaps we should say Judaeo-Christianity) is the only religious tradition we are able to view from an 'insider' perspective, which doesn't necessarily imply that we're 'believers' – as it happens, one of us is, and the other isn't.

With that said about the aims and limitations of our discussion of religious naturalism in this Element, we'll now embark on our two-poled conceptual investigation into religiousness and naturalist commitment. We'll commence (in Section 2) with the first pole, by considering what understandings of 'being religious' may be held by those advocating a religious attitude towards the natural world. This will enable us to distinguish between relatively 'thin' and relatively 'thick' ways in which naturalists may be religious. 'Thinner' religious naturalisms keep within a scientific naturalist perspective, while 'thicker', more robust, ways of being religious involve metaphysical claims which go beyond anything science could admit. The possibility of more robust forms of religious naturalism, then, depends on what the commitments of 'naturalism' are taken to be, and what it could mean to claim that the natural world 'is all there is' – thereby leading us into the second pole of our conceptual investigation (in Section 3).

2 Understanding the *Religiousness* of Religious Naturalism

We start, then, with the idea that being a religious naturalist is a matter of having, and acting from, a religious orientation towards the natural world or some key aspect of it, such as nature's creativity. In what ways could such a stance count as 'religious'? As descriptive terms, 'religion' and 'religious' are what Ludwig Wittgenstein called 'family resemblance' concepts. We cannot define religion in terms of a single set of necessary and sufficient properties. Instead, religions exhibit an overlapping or criss-crossing set of similarities and affinities without there being any specifiable 'essence' of religion. Nevertheless, humanities and human sciences, such as history, sociology, and anthropology, study religions and religious phenomena, and the study of religion is itself an important disciplinary area. In practice, then, there are ways of demarcating its subject matter even though an essentialist definition of religion is not to be had. A functional approach often comes to the fore, in which religion is characterized in terms of typical functions that religious practices, attitudes, and beliefs play in the life of human communities. Certainly, this functional approach is important for philosophical discussions of religion, where the *normative* question arises whether religion has a place in the best ways of human living, and, if so, what the functions of religion are which give it its place in human flourishing. Philosophers, then, in pursuing the question 'How should we live?', may propose *a normative definition of ideal religion* – a definition of the kind of religion that, in their view, contributes to living life well, collectively as well as individually.

In considering what is religious about religious naturalism, we'll follow this normative approach. After all, religious naturalists recommend their perspective on reality as something good which may even be necessary if humans are to flourish in, and with, their environment. In what sense of 'religious', then, does a religious naturalist option count as 'religious'? Since religious naturalism is concerned with living well in our environment, the question arises whether 'being religious' need amount here only to following an environmental *ethics* that affirms nature-friendly virtues and ideals, such as conservation and the sustainable use of resources. What reason could there be to value *specifically religious* attitudes to nature above, or in addition to, those recommended by an adequate environmental ethics? In this section, we'll distinguish different grades of religiousness that may characterize this type of religious naturalism, arising from differing answers to this question – answers which differ in how much they expect a religious perspective to offer beyond purely ethical content.

2.1 Religious Feelings in Response to Nature's Sacredness

One possible view is to accept that the practical content of religious naturalism is no more than a set of nature-friendly moral ideals. Calling commitment to those ideals 'religious' may then be justified in so far as it is accompanied by subjective feelings and attitudes towards nature of the kind valorized in religious traditions, such as awe, reverence, and gratitude, as well as by a tendency to describe *the world itself* in terms correlated with such feelings. Religious naturalists speak, for example, of *nature's* sacredness, holiness, or, in some cases, of its being divine or containing divinity. Feelings of reverence towards nature are thus viewed as subjective *responses* to something of great worth attributed to the natural world itself.

This idea of a religious response to the sacred worth of, or in, nature can be interpreted philosophically in two contrasting ways. The first – more obvious – way is to hold that human responses of wonder, reverence, and thankfulness are responses to what is objectively 'there' in the natural world itself, independently of whether or not humans experience and respond to it. On this 'realist' account, humans *ought to* respond to nature in religious ways; reverence and gratitude are the apt or right responses to nature's *intrinsic* sacred worth.

Realism about values in general is, however, a common target of philosophical scepticism, especially amongst those who think of themselves as committed to naturalism: how could anything have worth other than in relation to its being valued by conscious beings with desires and preferences? Naturalist 'value-anti-realism' comes in several varieties – for example, non-cognitivism, for which (roughly) evaluative utterances express preferences or implicit commands rather than truth-claims, and fictionalists who hold (roughly) that evaluative facts are useful fictions.[6] Some naturalists would accommodate evaluative facts by noting that, for example, the disposition to produce (under certain conditions) human religious feelings and attitudes is a real enough 'response-dependent' property of features of the natural world. But that property falls short of the property of *requiring* such responses from minds with a human-type psychology, which is what is needed if, as a full-blooded realist will insist, nature (or some key feature of it) has sacred worth *intrinsically*, independently even of the very existence of humans or similar beings. A religious naturalism that adopts a less than fully realist interpretation of the religiously significant worth that resides in nature is, we suggest, religious only in a relatively 'thin' sense. A 'thicker' grade of religious naturalism regards human attitudes of reverence towards nature as apt responses to the sacred value that nature has intrinsically. On this fully realist view, what is revered in nature is revered because it is sacred; it is not sacred because humans have religious feelings towards it.

Taking nature's sacredness to be a real intrinsic property yields a grade of religious naturalism that is 'thicker' in the sense that it is metaphysically bolder than alternative less fully realist views. The question arises whether this bolder metaphysical commitment coheres with a naturalist stance. Perhaps a naturalist

---

[6] Non-cognitivism seems much less fashionable nowadays than it used to be. But see Mark van Roojen's (2023) discussion of varieties of non-cognitivism and borderline cases of it. 'Fictionalism' about a range of discourse (including moral, mathematical, scientific, modal, and religious) is increasingly popular, though it has meant a number of different things. For a general discussion of fictionalism, i.e., not focusing on fictionalism about a specific discourse, see, e.g., Matti Eklund (2024).

can be religious only by being metaphysically cautious and taking nature's sacred worth to be something humanly conferred on nature, or, anyway, something non-intrinsic whose reality is essentially linked to actual and potential human responses? We'll return to this question later, since the answer depends on what 'naturalism' may be taken to mean – and that's the focus of the second pole of our conceptual investigation of the idea of a religious naturalism (see Section 3). For now, we'll continue with the first pole, exploring further how to understand the religiousness of a religious naturalism that takes a fully realist religious view of the sacredness of nature.

2.2 Religious Naturalism: 'Grounding' an Eco-Morality

Religious naturalisms that take nature (or some aspect of it) as their religious object typically affirm an 'eco-morality' which includes nature-friendly moral ideals (that is, ideals about how humans should relate rightly to their natural environment and its resources, as well as ideals about right relationships amongst humans). 'Thicker' forms of religious naturalism take the 'moral realist' view that their ideals are 'objectively' right, and not just right relatively to human preferences or social and cultural traditions, as 'moral anti-realists' hold. In addition – and this is important – fully realist religious naturalisms claim that the objective rightness of nature-friendly ideals is 'grounded' in *ultimate* reality. They hold, that is, that it is *because* nature ultimately possesses the religiously significant worth that it does that a specific objective eco-morality applies.

An appeal to 'ultimates' is a characteristic feature of religious worldviews.[7] But what exactly does it mean to say that the ideals of eco-morality have ultimate grounds in the sacred worth of nature? Broadly speaking, the idea of an ultimate is the idea of a certain kind of limit – to put it colloquially, an idea about 'where the buck stops'. Religious claims about ultimates are claims about 'where the buck stops' *explanatorily* – namely, in something whose ultimate reality can explain why other things are as they are, while needing no explanation beyond itself for its own reality. Realist religious naturalism treats nature's sacredness as just such an ultimate, from which both right attitudes and right ways of human living in the natural environment derive.

---

[7] John Schellenberg argues that we need to think of religion as potentially evolving into an indefinitely lengthy future from its current forms and, in that context, he characterizes religious worldviews as affirming 'ultimates' of (up to) three kinds – 'metaphysical', 'axiological', and 'soteriological'. He uses the term 'ultimism' to refer to religious worldviews that posit a transcendent reality that is ultimate in all three of these ways. See, e.g., Schellenberg (2016: 166).

There is a contrast, then, with purely ethical attempts to ground the ideals of an eco-morality. Secular or humanist naturalists may claim that they can derive an adequate environmental ethics – for example, on the basis of broad utilitarian considerations that include the utilities of future generations and of sentient beings other than humans.[8] It's a pertinent question whether a religious naturalism that affirms the ultimate sacred worth of nature offers more secure foundations for eco-morality than any purely ethical theory such as utilitarianism. To answer that question, and to make it intelligible how a religious perspective on nature's ultimate reality could ground an eco-morality, we would need some account of what ultimately *constitutes* nature's sacred worth – a topic we'll consider later (see Section 4). It's enough for now to appreciate that one kind of religiousness that a religious naturalism may exhibit is the kind of religiousness that not only affirms a value-realist morality but also grounds that morality on the foundations of a religious account of ultimate reality.

2.3 Natural Reality as Ultimately Favourable to the Pursuit of an Eco-Morality

We have distinguished relatively thin, metaphysically cautious, forms of religious naturalism from thicker, metaphysically bolder forms. 'Thin' religious naturalisms take nature's sacredness to be essentially related to human responses, yet something in which it is important to believe because this has beneficial consequences for human flourishing in harmony with the environment. On a 'thin' view, eco-moral ideals are not 'grounded' in any intrinsic features of ultimate reality. Even if some value-realist view is taken of those ideals themselves, a 'thin' account takes nature's religiously significant features to be either mere projections of human attitudes, or, anyway, dependent on actual or potential human responses to reality. By contrast, 'thicker', fully realist, forms of religious naturalism (if they are possible) would offer a metaphysics of ultimate, but still 'natural', reality from which the correctness of its eco-ideals and the aptness of religious attitudes towards nature derive. This would yield for religious naturalism something beyond its purely moral content – namely, a secure basis for moral ideals in the nature of ultimate reality.

But religion characteristically plays a further role in affirming that reality is, so to speak, ultimately *favourable to* the pursuit by human beings of (what it takes to be) the right moral ideals. Religion tells us that the way things ultimately are makes it reasonable to commit ourselves to living in accordance

---

[8] For a general survey of utilitarianism, see, e.g., Julia Driver (2022). For an attempt to promote a utilitarian theory of climate ethics, see John Broome (2012). For some doubts about the extent to which a utilitarian ethic can also be an environmental ethic, see, e.g., Andrew Brennan and Norva Lo (2024, section 4).

with certain moral ideals. It tells us that we may pursue those ideals *hopefully*, even when faced with obstacles and failures. Religions that fulfil this function posit a metaphysics of ultimate reality that grounds not only certain ideals but also the hope that living in accordance with those ideals is the path to human fulfilment (that is, to the satisfaction of our ultimate interests, not just individually but also as social groups within the wider environment). Sticking to the right ideals is often costly, requiring us to confront adversaries, and to set aside other desires – maybe, at the extreme, to the point of sacrificing one's life. Furthermore, we often fail to meet our ideals though we still endorse them, even when following them would have been easy enough, and we may come to despair at our own weakness, self-absorption, and moral failures. Obstacles to pursuing our ideals come from within ourselves as well as from outside. In grounding the hope that trying to live by its ideals is the path to human fulfilment, a religious metaphysics of ultimate reality that performs this function provides a *soteriology* – a means for 'salvation' from the obstacles that threaten to undermine our ultimate human fulfilment. (Soteriology and salvation are to be understood here in a broad sense, not confined to Christian concepts such as sin and redemption, heaven and hell.)

In considering, then, what functions an ideal religion might serve in human existence, we may expect it to offer a metaphysics of ultimate reality that not only grounds moral ideals but also hope for ultimate human fulfilment through pursuit of those ideals and, as well, the means of 'salvation' from obstacles to that fulfilment. We'll describe as *robustly* religious those perspectives that make bold metaphysical claims of this kind. After considering different understandings of what may be meant by naturalism (Section 3), we'll go on (in Section 4) to consider how an outlook on reality which is still meaningfully naturalist can also be robustly religious by affirming an ultimate reality that grounds hopeful pursuit of an eco-morality.

2.4 A 'Religion of Nature'?

Before proceeding, though, it's worth raising the question whether religious naturalisms of the kind we've been discussing so far – namely, those that ascribe religious worth to nature or some key feature of it – would have to be associated with *an actual religion*, a 'religion of Nature', one might say. Some who see religious naturalism as a religious attitude towards nature insist that it is not 'a religion' (see, e.g., Hogue, 2014: 6). Some even hesitate to call it 'religious': Crosby (2003: 119), for example, prefers to call his version of religious naturalism 'naturism', because, for him, 'Nature in and of itself is … religiously ultimate'. And Goodenough (see 2023: 102) suggests that 'spiritual naturalism' may be a more accurate term for the perspective described in her book *The Sacred Depths of Nature*. It's a common feature of the decline of traditional religious affiliation in 'Western' societies for people who want to retain something valuable from the religion they now reject to say that they are 'spiritual', but not 'religious'. Being 'spiritual' somehow strikes people as not implying belief in anything supernatural in the way that being religious is usually assumed to do. And being spiritual also gets understood largely as a private thing, not requiring the membership of communities and institutions that is typical of traditional religions, nor engaging in their communal rites and observances.

It is an interesting question whether *the practice* of a religious outlook on reality must essentially be linked to a communal religious movement. Do religious naturalists need a 'religion of Nature'? Some who answer 'no' may, as just noted, downplay the religiousness of their stance. That may be because they sense that a genuinely religious stance *would* involve belonging to a religious movement that confers a shared identity. Being religious entirely by oneself seems difficult if not impossible: spiritual practices, even of solitary hermits, typically relate to the shared tradition of some communal fellowship. Perhaps, though, the fellowship to which one relates as a religious naturalist need have few if any of the usual trappings of religion, consisting in only a virtual community of the like-minded.[9] But if a religious naturalism is to fulfil the functions needed to be *robustly* religious, then some of the 'trappings' of religion may be practically very helpful, if not essential – for example, disciplined routines and communal rites focused on what is held to be of ultimate worth.[10] The question then arises where a 'religion of Nature' may already exist – or else, if it needs a fresh start, where resources may be found for developing its practices and beliefs. Religious naturalists often distance

---

[9] See, e.g., the website of the Religious Naturalist Association (formed in 2014): https://religious-naturalist-association.org/, which provides a range of activities (mostly online), including meetings, webinars, an online forum as well as a monthly newsletter and information about conferences that may be of interest. For 'a report from the field in 2017', see Ursula Goodenough, Michael Cavanaugh and Todd Macalister (2018). The Institute on Religion in an Age of Science (see www.iras.org/) has hosted annual conferences (since 1954) and (since 2020) has a monthly webinar series. Unitarian Universalist Religious Naturalists (see https://uurn.weebly.com/) was founded in 2004 to create a community of religious naturalists scattered throughout Unitarian Universalist congregations. The Spiritual Naturalist Society (see www.snsociety.org/), formed in 2012, promotes a range of synchronous and asynchronous online interactions for like-minded people from all traditions.

[10] Eric Steinhart (2018) says that religious naturalism needs to develop systems of practices that encourage living in accordance with its core values and discusses different strategies for doing this. Loyal Rue (2011: 135) observes that 'All religious naturalists are united by a reverence for nature, but they are not united by any distinctive patterns that might describe the[ir] worship life.' Todd Macalister (2021) gives an overview of the types of practices in which religious naturalists have said they are or could be engaged.

themselves from some aspects of their own inherited traditions, yet find other aspects inspirational for filling out a religious naturalist stance. We'll take up in Section 5 the question of what a robustly religious naturalism might draw from existing traditions – even to the extent of remaining within a tradition while developing or rediscovering its naturalist potential. But now we'll pursue our conceptual inquiry into religious naturalism by moving on to its second pole – namely, the question of what the naturalism of religious naturalism may mean.

3 Understanding the *Naturalism* of Religious Naturalism

Is a religious naturalism possible, and, if so, what sort of content might it offer as a live contemporary religious option? That is our leading question. A religious naturalist worldview would have to be naturalist in a meaningful sense. In this section we aim to consider what that may imply. As Philip Kitcher (2018: 66) has remarked, 'in the house of naturalism there are many mansions'. Many assume that 'naturalism' implies an explicitly non-religious worldview, since religion is thought to require something naturalism rules out, namely supernatural agency.[11] A viable account of religious naturalism needs to dissolve this apparent contradiction. We'll consider, then, what 'naturalism' may reasonably be taken to mean: are there forms of naturalism consistent with a genuinely religious perspective? Is there, in particular, conceptual space for a form of naturalism which is robustly religious in the way described above in Section 2.3 – namely, in positing a metaphysics of ultimate reality that grounds ideals which include nature-friendly values and which also has a 'hope-grounding' and broadly soteriological component? Or must we conclude that a naturalism that deserves the name can be 'religious' only in a thinner, metaphysically more cautious, sense?

3.1 'Nature is All That There is': Naturalism as 'One-World-ism'

Naturalism is connected with the idea of 'the natural world'. In some contexts, the 'natural' world is contrasted with the 'human' world, the world of society and culture. No such contrast is intended here. Rather, speaking of the 'natural' world – of which humans and human societies and cultures are a part – here implies a contrast with the possibility of a world which is *not* natural because it

---

[11] Defenders of this view, for varying reasons, include Daniel Dennett (2006: 9), Richard Dawkins (2006: 19), Alvin Plantinga (2011: ix), Ronald Dworkin (2013: 12–13), and Graham Oppy (2018: ch. 4). Dworkin (2013) describes his view as 'religious' – but as a 'religious atheism' rather than a 'religious naturalism', since he thinks that the 'religious attitude' and 'naturalism' are diametrically opposed. For Dworkin, the 'religious attitude' is at a relatively 'thick' position on the spectrum of what we've said 'being religious' might mean, insofar as he seems to see value as an objective, independent, fundamental feature of reality.

is 'above' nature (*super*-natural) or 'beyond' nature (*supra*-natural). The Abrahamic religious traditions, with their concept of God as creator and the natural world as God's creation, are widely understood as 'supernaturalist' – that is, as committed to the idea of a supernatural order distinct from, though interacting with, 'the natural order'. Religious *naturalism* may thus be understood to mean a religious worldview that rejects any ontological order beyond or above the natural world, and therefore holds that *there is no world but the natural world*. Defending the possibility of a *religious* naturalism accordingly depends on successfully explaining how an identifiably religious perspective could accept that, as Crosby (2013: 744) puts it, 'Nature in some shape or form is all there is now, ever has been, and ever shall be'.

But what does it mean to say that 'Nature is all that there is'? A straightforward answer is that this claim affirms a 'one-world' ontology as against the 'two-world' ontology familiar from a standard understanding of Abrahamic theism. According to that standard understanding, God is a personal being who is the creator ex nihilo of all else that exists. God is thus an *uncreated* being. God must therefore belong to a distinct ontological category from the natural world of created beings. On this account, then, naturalism amounts to the *one-world-ist* claim that there is no other world but the one natural world, no beings other than natural beings. (This claim may be qualified as applying only to concrete as opposed to abstract reality by those who hold that abstract entities, such as numbers and propositions, need to be accepted as real though they don't belong to the contingent natural world.)

Religious naturalism can therefore mean a religious perspective which affirms the 'one-world' ontology of a single natural world. Such a perspective views existence as a unified whole. That's a religiously appealing idea, suggested, perhaps, by the etymology of 'religion' (if that term does derive, as often claimed, from the Latin *religere*, 'to bind together'). As Wittgenstein avers in his *Tractatus Logico-Philosophicus*, 'Feeling the world as a limited whole – it is this that is mystical' (1961 [1922]: §6.45). Pantheist religious sensibility expresses the same idea, identifying the divine not as the mere sum total of existents but as their constituting an 'all-inclusive unity'.[12]

This one-world-ist formulation differs from the formulation of religious naturalism with which we began. That formulation characterized religious naturalism as a matter of having religious attitudes towards nature and taking

---

[12] Alasdair MacIntyre (1967: 34) describes pantheism as the view that 'everything that exists is a unity and ... the all-inclusive unity is divine'. For an extensive discussion of the different senses of what may be or has been meant by 'unity' and 'divinity' in a pantheist context, see Michael Levine (1994: ch. 2). We'll remark further on pantheist views as related to religious naturalism in Section 5.3.

the natural world itself (or some aspect of it) as the object of ultimate religious worth – a view which, from now on, we'll refer to as *naturist*.[13] What is the relation between these two kinds of religious naturalism – *naturist* and *one-world-ist*? It seems possible to be a one-world-ist religious naturalist without being a naturist religious naturalist. That is, a religious perspective might hold that there is no world but the natural world *without* taking the natural world (or anything in it) as its object of ultimate religious worth. This would be the case, for example, for a worldview that retains the Abrahamic concept of God on some alternative to the standard understanding noted earlier in this section, yet without identifying God with Nature or any part of it. (For more on one-world-ist religious naturalisms that are not 'naturist', see Section 5.3.)

Naturist religious naturalists characteristically *also* hold the one-world-ist conviction that the natural world, which provides the object of their religious attitudes, is all that there is or could be. That's hardly surprising: if the ultimate object of your religious concern is Nature or within nature, you have no religious reason to posit anything beyond nature. One-worldist religious naturalism is thus best seen as a genus of which naturist religious naturalism is a species, leaving it open that there may be other species of one-world-ist religious naturalism whose object of ultimate religious concern is neither nature as a whole nor any core feature of nature.

3.2 Specifying 'the Natural World'

Just what is meant by 'the natural world'? We've used the phrase often, but without fully specifying its meaning. One-world-ist naturalism – the thesis that there is but one world, namely, the natural world – makes a determinate claim only given a specification of what the natural world is. And the possibility of (various forms of) one-world-ist *religious* naturalism needs to be judged relative to assumptions about what the natural world, on a given specification of it, may and may not include. What specification of the natural world may we give, then, without already building in any religious assumptions (such as identifying nature as God's creation, as in Abrahamic theism)?

---

[13] Our use of 'naturist' follows Crosby (2003: 119), who, as noted in Section 2.4, uses the term for a religious naturalism that takes Nature as religiously ultimate. Crosby builds into his use of 'naturism' his own preference for rejecting all concepts of God, gods, or divinity. But, as we are using the term, a naturist perspective might deploy such concepts, but only provided one of the following applies: (i) God (capital-G) is identified with Nature itself or something within it, and/or gods (small-g) are identified as beings or energies within the natural world; or (ii) talk of God (capital-G) is understood in a symbolic or metaphorical ('anti-realist') way as facilitating commitment to the religious ultimacy of Nature or something within it.

A religiously neutral place to start would seem to be with the idea that the natural world is the world as disclosed to human beings through our sensory experience. That includes, of course, not only our external perceptions but also our inner reflections and proprioceptions: we humans are ourselves part of the world disclosed to us in sensory experience. May we identify that experienced world as the natural world, which the naturalist says is 'all that there is'? Hardly! Our sensory powers are limited, so there may be more to reality than we have it within our powers to perceive through the senses. That's an important truth – but it opens a Pandora's box of potential appeals to non-sensory modes of intuition and revelations of spiritual and religious reality. Unless some limits may be placed on such appeals, the possibility is undermined of a shared, religiously neutral, conception of 'the natural world'.

A ('Western') scientific approach promises to keep the lid on this Pandora's box by rescuing a determinate, supposedly neutral, conception of the natural world. Under a scientific approach, what belongs to the natural world may readily be extended from what we may immediately perceive to include things perceivable only with the assistance of instruments such as microscopes and telescopes. In addition, scientific explanatory theories typically posit theoretical entities (subatomic particles, for example) – and these, too, may be regarded as belonging to the natural world. Such theories remain tethered to what we can perceive, since they may be confirmed only on the evidence of our publicly checkable sensory perceptual experience.

A determinate conception of 'the natural world' thus emerges – namely, as the world experienced in sensory perception and able to be further understood only through empirically well-confirmed explanatory theories in the empirical sciences (including psychology and the social sciences, as well as the 'harder' sciences, biology, chemistry, and physics). Empirically well-confirmed scientific theories may be interpreted either in a realist or an anti-realist ('instrumentalist') way, according to whether the entities they posit are treated as real entities or only as useful tools for predicting and explaining observable phenomena.[14] Even on an instrumentalist account well-confirmed scientific theories enlarge our understanding of what the natural world is like beyond what we can perceive of it (if these theories 'work', the world, whatever it is like 'in itself', must be such as to make the relevant instrumental models of it apt).

One way of determining what counts as the natural world, then, is as the world as we sensorily perceive it enhanced *only* by what scientific theorizing can disclose – to the extent, that is, that the posits of such theorizing are confirmed

---

[14] For useful surveys of realist/anti-realist debates in science, see, e.g., Stathis Psillos (1999) and Anjan Chakravartty (2017).

in experience. If the natural world under *that* determination is the only world there is, then nothing is concretely (as opposed to abstractly) real unless its existence and properties are in principle knowable empirically through observationally-based methods of scientific inquiry. This claim is widely referred to as *scientific naturalism*.

Sensory perceptual-based methods of scientific inquiry deserve to be accepted as reliable routes to knowledge of reality – assuming, anyway, that an adequate response can be given to external world scepticism, and that suitable qualifications are made about the limits of empirical knowledge. Those qualifications include, first, that empirical, scientific, knowledge deals in probabilities rather than certainties; second, that scientific knowledge is in principle fallible, revisable in the light of future experience; and, third, that the development of bodies of scientific knowledge is conditioned by their historical and cultural situatedness. With all that said, we may affirm that science does convey understanding about what our world is like. But it's a distinct and bolder claim to hold that reality consists *only* in the ways those sense-based scientific routes to knowledge understand it – even when that claim is qualified as applying only to concrete reality.

Scientific inquiry is, of course, *methodologically* naturalist. *Methodological naturalism* specifies intrinsic limitations on the kinds of hypotheses that count as scientific. Properly scientific hypotheses must be empirically testable – testable, that is, against in principle publicly checkable sensory-based observations. Furthermore, properly scientific hypotheses treat the world we experience through sensory perception as 'causally closed'. This is the 'one-world-ism' that is intrinsic to the scientific method: any hypothesis about what causally explains some phenomenon in the world is intrinsically a hypothesis about some features of, or events or processes that occur in, that very same world.

However, science's *methodological* naturalism does not entail the *ontological* conclusion that there is nothing more to (concrete) reality than is disclosed by empirical scientific methods. Nor can empirical scientific methods themselves confirm such a claim. To upgrade methodological naturalism into an ontological thesis by claiming that there is nothing concretely real beyond what would feature in a notionally completed natural scientific description of the world is to go beyond empirical science into contestable metaphysics. It is therefore apt to refer to this thesis as '*metaphysical* naturalism'. As John Haught (2003: 770) succinctly puts it, 'Methodological naturalism maintains that *as far as scientific knowing is concerned*, nature is all that there is. Metaphysical naturalism, on the other hand, goes much farther, insisting that nature is literally all there is.'

Metaphysical naturalism uses the science-based conception of the natural world to specify what there is when 'nature is literally all that there is'. Of course, there is more to be said about exactly what limits the science-based conception places on what can count as belonging to the natural world. In particular, the question arises whether metaphysical naturalism implies physicalism – namely, the thesis that everything concretely real is physical in the sense that there is a true description of it in the language of fundamental physical theory (at least in principle, even if no such purely physical description could actually be accessed). If the scientifically disclosable world is taken to be causally closed *at the level of fundamental physical reality*, then the metaphysical scientific naturalist will be a physicalist in the sense just defined, ruling out the Cartesian view that consciousness belongs to a distinct non-physical ontological order somehow interacting with the bodily, physical, order. For present purposes, it's not important to go into the question whether a properly scientific naturalism could accept mind/body dualism. But it is important to note that metaphysical scientific naturalism doesn't need to deny 'immaterial' realities, even if it does entail physicalism. This is because it may be accepted that physical reality, in its complex developed forms, has emergent properties – such as life, consciousness, and agency – and that there are autonomous sciences (biology, psychology) that deal with properties at these emergent levels and whose content cannot be reduced to purely physical content, even though what ultimately constitutes living and conscious beings are complexly organized physical systems.[15]

3.3 Religious Naturalism and Scientific Metaphysical Naturalism

How do religious naturalisms stand in relation to the metaphysical scientific naturalist claim that the natural world – which naturalism claims is all that there is – is nothing more or less than the world as science can know it to be?

As noted in Section 1, one main motivation for religious naturalism is a desire for forms of religion that 'take science seriously'. Religious naturalisms, then, need a worldview which coheres with well-confirmed empirical scientific theories. This constraint entails that, since scientific theoretical accounts of the world change and develop, and could never reach any state of final certainty, religious naturalisms cannot take any stance that could not adapt to shifts in

---

[15] Our characterization of metaphysical scientific naturalism as the claim that the one natural world is just the world as science can know it thus amounts to what Fiona Ellis (2014) calls 'expansive scientific naturalism': whatever, and only whatever, empirical scientific methods can disclose belongs to the natural world. More restricted forms of metaphysical scientific naturalism have been espoused by some philosophers. Following David Macarthur's (2010) terminology, 'extreme scientific naturalism' holds that the limits of nature are circumscribed by the limits of physics alone, and 'narrow scientific naturalism' holds that those limits are set by the 'hard' sciences (physics, chemistry, and biology). 'Broad scientific naturalism' allows that the human/social sciences as well as the 'hard' sciences can disclose natural realities; and it is that broader version that we intend when we speak of metaphysical scientific naturalism.

scientific understanding. Accordingly, religious naturalisms may make posits about ultimate reality only if taking them as foundational could not in principle conflict with scientific developments.

Religious naturalists share with metaphysical scientific naturalists the claim that our world is *one* world: they are, as already argued, *one-world-ist* naturalists. Science itself can't rule out two-world-ist metaphysical schemes. That can be done only by taking a certain metaphysical stance, as do some (though by no means all) *philosophers* of science – namely, those who are *metaphysical* scientific naturalists. Religious naturalists take the metaphysical stance that there is no (concrete) world but the natural world. And some – but *only* some – religious naturalists take a further step by committing to *the metaphysical scientific naturalist understanding* of what the natural world is. These religious naturalists often see this commitment as *itself* a religious one: it is the natural world existing by itself *just as science can reveal it* that inspires their awe and reverence.[16]

Metaphysical scientific naturalists do not generally accept that the feelings they may have about nature involve anything religious. Nevertheless, their worldview is sometimes presented in quasi-religious ways, and may be associated with movements sociologically similar to religious ones – for example, the 'brights' network, and the 'evolutionary consciousness' movement inspired by the works of Richard Dawkins.[17] Anything genuinely religious in these movements should (for self-consistency) involve only the thinner, less realist, forms of religion that remain within the limits of metaphysical scientific naturalism. The more that a 'spirituality' is associated with a scientific naturalist view of the world, the more pressure there seems to be on keeping within those limits. For example, Dawkins extols gratitude as an apt response to the chanciness of our individual existence on Darwinian evolutionary assumptions – although, of course, he doesn't think there is anyone or anything to which we owe our thankfulness. But if Dawkins' 'gratitude spirituality' extends to the idea that gratitude is an apt human response to intrinsically real features of the natural world, it implies a realist stance that breaks with metaphysical scientific naturalism and could count as naturalist only in some broader sense.[18]

And there *is* conceptual space for broader notions of naturalism that have an expanded view of what can count as 'within' the one natural world. *One-world-ist naturalism does not entail metaphysical scientific naturalism*. The one world that we can know through sensory perceptual-based scientific methods may also include real features which cannot be known in that way. A one-world-ist

---

[16] On the role of awe and wonder in scientific practice, see Helen de Cruz (2020).
[17] See www.the-brights.net and www.richarddawkins.net.
[18] See Bishop (2010) for further discussion.

naturalism can thus be an 'expansive' naturalism.[19] For example, Graham Oppy (2018) takes naturalism to be expansive enough to be value-realist – that is, to include the 'mind-independent' reality of values, something that metaphysical scientific naturalism seems to rule out, allowing that values have real existence only essentially in relation to valuing minds. Oppy argues that naturalism, though it may admit mind-independent values, cannot admit any religiously realist metaphysics. For Oppy, naturalism entails that there are no non-natural causal agents or non-natural causal regulative structures, but (on his view) a religiously realist metaphysics requires belief in just such agents or regulative structures.

Fiona Ellis (e.g., 2014, 2019, 2020, and 2022) goes further than admitting mind-independent values as belonging to the one natural world. She promotes a version of 'theistic expansive naturalism', which opens the door wider to include religious realisms that enhance the one natural world yet without positing any concrete supernatural ontological order.[20] That's the degree of expansion needed to make space for the more robustly religious naturalism we have earlier described – namely, a religious naturalism that posits a one-world metaphysics of ultimate reality that grounds, not only nature-friendly moral ideals but also the hope that pursuit of those ideals, despite adversities and failures, is the key to human fulfilment in harmony with the wider environment.

3.4 Taking Science Seriously: A Constraint on Expansive Naturalism

There is conceptual space, then, for an expansive one-world-ist religious naturalism with a non-supernaturalist metaphysics that functions to ground ideals and support some form of soteriology. But how expansive could a religious worldview be while remaining meaningfully 'naturalist'? What kinds of 'expansions' are admissible? One-world-ism doesn't seem sufficient for naturalism: one might imaginatively populate the one natural world with many enchanted things that go beyond anything a naturalist could admit yet without implying any radical supernatural/natural dualism.

As we've noted, to be 'naturalist' a worldview must not only be one-world-ist, it must also take science seriously. But what does this additional condition mean? Taking science seriously must at least imply proper respect for empirical evidence in settling factual matters. But how are we to show that proper respect?

---

[19] Another term often used is 'liberal naturalism'. Liberal naturalism lies somewhere in the conceptual space between metaphysical scientific naturalism and supernaturalism. It is usually assumed to stop short of any sort of religious or theistic naturalism. For further discussion of liberal naturalism, see, e.g., Mario De Caro and David Macarthur (2010 and 2022).

[20] Evidently, if such religious realisms can be theist, the question arises what conception of God could be consistent with a one-world-ist stance. We'll return to this question in Section 5.3.

A common assumption is that to do so requires committing to the truth of the foundational claims of a worldview only to the extent that the available evidence supports their truth.

Now, the practical impact of following that rule depends on what may be admitted as relevant evidence. Scientific methods require evidence to rest on checkable perceptual observations. If that's the sort of evidence that's required, the scope for religious worldviews that take science seriously seems narrow. It's true that, during the European Enlightenment, empirical arguments for God's existence were championed – in particular, the 'design argument'. This has been revived as the 'new' teleological argument which argues for the existence of a supreme intelligence from the 'fine-tuning' of the Universe's physical constants to allow for the emergence of conscious intelligent life. In the Enlightenment, the project of empirically 'proving' God's existence was known as 'natural religion': it's the subject of David Hume's critique in his *Dialogues Concerning Natural Religion* (1993 [1779]). The success of 'natural theology' (as it is now more commonly known) continues to be disputed. But, even if, say, the argument from fine-tuning succeeds (which we believe it does not),[21] the supreme intelligence whose existence it made empirically probable would – simply as a consequence of science's methodological naturalism – count as something within the closed causal system of the natural world, and that would arguably limit its specifically religious significance.

If a naturalist worldview that 'takes science seriously' must confine itself to empirically confirmed foundations, then a naturalist worldview could be religious only in the 'thin' ways consistent with metaphysical caution. But a less restrictive interpretation may be placed on 'taking science seriously'. Certainly, empirical evidence must be respected in settling factual questions; but taking science seriously also involves recognizing its limitations. One limitation is that, though it's 'Western' science that naturalists typically want to take seriously, bodies of experience-based knowledge are found also in non-Western traditions and Indigenous cultures. Given that all scientific knowledge is in principle open to revision and paradigm change, some 'non-Western' knowledge currently thought less than 'properly scientific' might come to be more integrated into a future scientific view of the world.[22]

---

[21] Some (though not usually philosophers) challenge the claim that the universe is *fine-tuned* for *life*. More deny that the hypothesis of God as intelligent designer is genuinely explanatory, or (even if it were) they say it is not the best explanation. For many, a multiverse (together with the weak anthropic principle) offers a better, if not the best, explanation. Some think the standard presentations of the fine-tuning argument are based on fallacious probability reasoning. For this criticism, see Mark Colyvan et al. (2005).

[22] For example, in recent years, there has been a growing recognition in the West of health care approaches that are not typically part of conventional (i.e., Western) medicine, such as

A second limitation, highly salient for religious worldviews, is that claims about how reality *ultimately* is – in itself, *independently* of how we experience it – cannot in principle be settled just by appeal to empirical evidence. Nevertheless, these are *factual* claims.[23] If, as widely agreed, factual claims cannot be settled a priori, it follows that claims about ultimate reality may be accepted only if it is sometimes reasonable to commit to the truth of a proposition 'beyond the evidence' as a matter of faith.

Now, some ('evidentialists') will insist that faith going beyond the evidence is always unreasonable. For them, both 'scientistic' commitment to the idea that the natural world has to be just the scientifically knowable world, and commitments to any of the various religious expansions of that world, are equally irrational and 'ideological'. Of course, religious believers may find their beliefs supported by their personal, subjective, experience. But this type of evidence is a matter more of emotional and spiritual than sensory perceptual experience, and it counts as evidence only when already interpreted from a 'believing' perspective. Religious beliefs *are* supported by religious experience – and that can be vitally important for continued religious commitment. But this kind of evidential support is not scientifically adequate because it doesn't count as independent evidence acceptable as such from the point of view of any inquirer.

Commitments to the truth of metaphysical claims about ultimate reality therefore require a *faith venture*. In 'The Will to Believe', William James proposed a justification of faith in just this sense – as practical commitment to truth-claims without the support of adequate scientifically admissible forms of evidence. James (1956 [1897]: 11) restricted justified faith to claims whose truth 'cannot *by its nature* be decided on intellectual grounds' (our emphasis). He thought it reasonable to take a stance on existentially vital questions such as the objective reality of values, and the meaningfulness or purposiveness of existence, even though intellectual arguments and scientifically admissible evidence could not even in principle settle the truth on questions like these. These kinds of questions are what Willem Drees calls 'limit' questions (see, e.g., Drees 1996: 18) – questions about the ultimate nature of the whole of reality, its existence and structure, questions on which religion characteristically ventures substantive answers.

---

acupuncture and yoga. Such 'non-mainstream' practices, rarely taken seriously in the past, have been increasingly used alongside or in combination with conventional Western medicine, and are thus often regarded as 'complementary' (rather than 'alternative'), forming part of what is nowadays called 'integrative health'.

[23] Pace the early to mid-twentieth century logical positivists, who thought that metaphysical claims about ultimate reality were factually meaningless because they are empirically neither verifiable nor falsifiable. See, e.g., A. J. Ayer (1952). It is now widely agreed that this kind of demarcation principle for factual meaningfulness cannot be successfully defended.

Commitment to a religious naturalism of a robust, metaphysically adventurous, kind would therefore require justification as a faith-venture, since its metaphysical content would augment a purely scientific view of reality. This needn't open Pandora's box, however, because James's restriction can be applied: venturing 'by faith' is admissible only on vital questions *in principle* unable to be settled by intellectual weighing of relevant evidence. All 'ordinary' factual questions are to be left unsettled if the evidence doesn't decide. A reasonable faith-venture must therefore be *consistent with* scientific resolution of all those questions that can be settled in this way. Religious one-world-ist naturalisms accept this constraint – and for good one-world-ist reasons. If the world of our experience is one, ultimately unified, world, then our understanding of what it is like and how it works should *itself* be integrated. The answers we accept by faith to religiously salient 'limit' questions, though necessarily going beyond well-confirmed scientific understandings of reality, must nevertheless cohere with those understandings.

3.5 Taking Stock

We've now explored both poles of our conceptual investigation into the possibility of religious naturalism. In Section 2, we saw that the religiousness of religious naturalists could be more or less metaphysically restrained or ambitious. On a restrained account, a 'thin' religious naturalism may rest its religiousness on religious feelings towards the natural world, with a property such as nature's sacredness understood as a projected or response-dependent property. Or, towards the more ambitious end of the spectrum, a robust religious naturalism may posit an ultimate reality that grounds nature-friendly values and makes it reasonable to pursue them, despite adversities, in the hope that so doing will lead to ultimate human fulfilment.

In Section 3, we noted that the natural world – the world we belong to and experience through our senses – may be further specified as the world known through scientific methods. Metaphysical scientific naturalism says that 'nature is all that there is' means that the natural world is neither more nor less than the world as can be known to science. We have argued, however, that one may be authentically naturalist by accepting that there is only one world, the natural world, *without* also accepting that science is the final arbiter of what belongs to that one natural world.

Religious naturalism has to strike a viable balance between its religious and its naturalist commitments. Metaphysically cautious and religiously restrained religious naturalism remains within the constraints of metaphysical scientific naturalism. But there is conceptual space for a bolder robustly religious naturalist metaphysics that augments a scientific view of the world yet remains naturalist – first, in affirming that there is only world, the natural world, and, second, in taking science seriously by going only beyond, not against, what our best scientific understanding of the world conveys. Commitment to such a robust religious one-world-ist naturalism – which may, or may not, be 'naturist', in taking Nature itself, or some core aspect of nature, as its religious ultimate – would require a faith-venture. But such a venture may be reasonable, given that it would provide an overall practical orientation to reality which grounds pursuit of nature-friendly ideals in the hope of human fulfilment, and is consistent with what our limited scientific methods tell us about our world.[24]

If we are right in our claim that there is conceptual space for an expansive naturalism that is religiously robust in the sense we've described, the question then arises whether that conceptual space is occupied. What kind of *content* could a metaphysically robust one-world-ist religious naturalism have?

4 Religious Naturalism and Cosmic Purposiveness

In this section, we will consider the claim that viable content for a robust one-world-ist religious naturalism may be provided by the claim that the natural world is purposive. To be more specific, the idea we'll explore is that the natural world is purposive in the sense that its existence has *an overall purpose*. This idea is often rejected by 'naturist' religious naturalists, who suspect that it has inevitable supernaturalist implications. But we think that, provided nature's overall purpose is held to be *inherent*, this idea (suitably developed) can provide the metaphysical basis for a robust religious naturalism.

4.1 Inherent Natural Purposes – Extendible to the Whole of Reality?

We have argued that a robust religious outlook posits an ultimate reality that grounds moral ideals plus the hope that commitment to those ideals can provide ultimate fulfilment and 'salvation' from obstacles that oppose it. Typically, religions richly specify their ideals at a practical level, providing teachers and exemplars of virtuous living, prophets who warn of lapses, and habitual practices that point a path towards fulfilled individual, social, and ecological living. Religious worldviews thus presuppose that human existence is meaningful and purposive.[25] But they also typically recognize humanity's dependence on the

---

[24] For more discussion and defence of a 'Jamesian' pragmatist defence of faith-ventures beyond, but not against, what can be settled by appeal to publicly checkable empirical evidence, see Bishop (2007) and (2023).

[25] How about religions that proclaim ultimate 'emptiness', such as Mahayana or Zen Buddhism? They nevertheless assume that there's real point in coming to terms with emptiness (i.e., with the impermanence and lack of inherent independent existence of all things). They teach that this may

wider environment, and see the natural world itself as purposive. In some religious worldviews there is the idea that the natural world exists for an *overall* purpose – and that idea, we think, can provide a foundation for a more robustly religious naturalist understanding of ultimate reality.

But could the natural world have an *inherent* overall purpose without anything beyond it capable of conferring a purpose upon it? The idea of inherent natural purposes is familiar from Aristotelian naturalism, which has been undergoing a contemporary revival in ethics and ethically-driven metaphysics.[26] According to Aristotelian naturalism, things in the world have natures specific to their kinds, and, for each kind, there is a good whose realization is constituted by the fulfilment of the *telos* or purpose of a thing of that kind. In this Aristotelian teleology there is no implication that the ends or *telē* of natural things are the purposes of some creating mind or organizing intelligence. This kind of inherent teleology is therefore compatible with naturalism – in an expansive one-world-ist form, anyway. (Metaphysical scientific naturalists won't admit Aristotelian natures or natural ends, though they may allow that Darwinian evolutionary theory supports some natural teleological claims – for example, the claim that the purpose of the heart is to pump blood.)

Neo-Aristotelian moral thinking applies this kind of naturalism to human existence, deriving the virtues as the dispositions for thought and action needed for realizing the *telos* of humanity, which is described as 'happiness' or 'flourishing' (translating Aristotle's *eudaimonia*). Aristotle identifies this as both our 'most final' end and our supreme good. Aristotelian naturalism is not generally regarded as religious, though neo-Aristotelian moral thinking does appeal to something ultimate (as is typical for religiously based ethics). For the neo-Aristotelian, goodness of character and rightness of behaviour are rooted in what's needed to realize humanity's *telos*. Ethical ideals thus derive from what it is, ultimately, to fulfil the purpose of being human.

Inherent teleology of this Aristotelian kind may be deployed for a more distinctively religious – and religiously naturalist – role. Inherent teleology could be *all-encompassing*; that is, there might be an ultimate purpose inherently attaching to *being real as such*. On this bold proposal, existence is seen as purposive in the sense that there is an *overall* ultimate *telos* whose realization is what everything real is ultimately 'for' – and which constitutes the good *for reality as such and as a whole*. On such a view, the different purposes of, and the different goods for, each specific kind of thing are somehow integrated into the

---

be done by reducing one's own suffering and showing compassion for the suffering of all other sentient beings. For a discussion of the meaningfulness of human life in Buddhism, especially in light of the Buddha's 'no-self' doctrine, see, e.g., Christopher Gowans (2018).

[26] See, e.g., Rosalind Hursthouse (1999) and Michael Thompson (2008).

overall ultimate purpose of, and the ultimate good for, reality itself and, thus, the whole natural cosmos.[27]

This vision – of an ultimate cosmic teleology – seems capable in principle of providing foundations for a robust religious perspective on ultimate reality which supports moral ideals and hope for fulfilment in pursuing them. Reality's ultimate purpose as posited by an all-encompassing inherent teleology would have to be the supreme good. The *telos* for something of a given kind is a conditioned good, and there can be things for which achieving their conditioned telic goods in a given circumstance would not be good (knives being used as murder weapons is a classic example). But the good *for reality as such* would be the supreme unconditioned good (since anything real that might be supposed to condition that good must itself exist essentially for the sake of that very same good). Thus, the right ideals for human existence will be the ideals that promote humanity's contributing to and participating in realizing that supreme good. Furthermore, living by those ideals will amount to living in accordance with reality's ultimate purpose, thus potentially grounding human hope for fulfilment by so doing. Of course, to get a sense of the viability of such a metaphysical basis for ethical ideals some specification for the supreme good will be needed – an issue we'll pursue in Section 5. But, first, we'll say more about the coherence of the idea of inherent cosmic purpose and how it may fit an expansive one-world-ist religious naturalism.

4.2 Naturalist Reservations about Ultimate Cosmic Purpose

Visions of ultimate cosmic teleology are often roundly rejected by religious naturalists. As Crosby (2003: 118) says, for example: 'Nature has no overarching, all-inclusive purpose or goal.' He adds 'while nature has no purpose, there is abundant manifestation of purpose *within* nature, i.e. in the outlooks and actions of purposive beings'. The reasons for this rejection are understandable.

For one thing, Aristotelian teleology may seem scientifically ruled out altogether ever since Newtonian physics displaced Aristotelian physics. It is commonly assumed that the shift to a mechanistic view in which final causes were subsumed under efficient causes resulted in the overall demise of teleology

---

[27] It is controversial whether we find in Aristotle's writings the idea of an *overall* good/*telos* in addition to the *telē* for the kinds of things (substantial natures) there are in the natural world. For an interesting discussion of cosmic teleology in Aristotle, see Monte Ransome Johnson (2005: ch. 9). Johnson concludes that an overall good or purpose is not an Aristotelian notion. Perhaps, however, this judgment is predicated on the assumption that one is asking whether there is a *single* good amongst the many different goods that could be the overall *telos*. But what we have in mind here (see Section 5.1 for more details) is an *integrative* good, not a single good that stands atop some hierarchy of goods and whose supremacy potentially competes with other goods.

in science. However, contemporary natural science is still open to teleology, especially in biology, and perhaps even in physics.[28]

But, even if there are scientific uses for the idea of things being 'for' some purpose, the idea of an ultimate purpose for reality as such is not something science could either confirm or disconfirm. If nature is all there is and we are part of nature, there could be no vantage point from which we might discern an overall purpose for reality. There could be no boundary that somehow contains nature and from (or outside of) which one might get a 'God's eye view'. So, the idea of an *overall cosmic purpose* can have no status as a meaningful scientific hypothesis. This is one reason why naturalists (including, seemingly, most religious naturalists) reject the notion of an overall cosmic purpose, thinking that it makes no sense.[29]

However, from a specific religious perspective the inherent directedness of everything upon an ultimate *telos* might be coherently 'read into' what science does confirm about the world. It is widely thought that such a vision of cosmic teleology belongs solely to the Abrahamic monotheist traditions. And those traditions are widely understood as positing a supernatural being who is creator of the cosmos. It is usually assumed, as Dubs (1943: 263) puts it, that 'without conscious foresight there can be no true purpose'. On this assumption, there can be a cosmic purpose only if there is a supreme agent who produces the cosmos to achieve that agent's intended purpose. But if the cosmos is all that there is, there can be no agent existing independently of and 'prior' to it. This is the second main reason why naturalists (again, including most religious naturalists) reject the notion of an overall cosmic purpose.[30]

For the idea of a cosmic purpose to be *religiously* useful, it must somehow be disclosed to humans as a purpose relevant to human existence. This doesn't imply that the purpose has to be *wholly* human-focused. Indeed, a truly cosmic purpose

---

[28] For a discussion of the ineliminability of teleological notions from modern biological sciences, see, e.g., Colin Allen and Jacob Neal (2020), and Colin Allen, Marc Bekoff, and George Lauder's (1998) anthology. For a recent discussion of teleology in physics, see, e.g., Richard Brock and Kostas Kampourakis (2023). For a more general defence of irreducible teleology in the sciences, see Matthew Tugby (2024).

[29] See, e.g., Richard Corrington (2007: 503–4), who expresses agreement with Crosby's rejection of an inherent cosmic purpose. Corrington (1998: 169) says:

Paradoxically, for the true naturalist, it makes no sense to even talk of nature per se, as if it were a *discriminandum* or object over and against the self. It makes more sense to see the word 'nature' as functioning as a kind of precategory, rather than as a term that could have a contrast. ... The precategory of nature refers to whatever is in whatever way.

[30] For example, Jerome Stone (2003: 90) follows Rem Edwards's (1972: 133–41) and Charley Hardwick's (1996: 5–8) definition of (religious) naturalism, which emphasizes that nature needs no explanation beyond itself and 'may be understood without appeal to any kind of intelligence or purposive agent'. That claim is then assumed to imply the denial of the thesis 'that some form of cosmic teleology is metaphysically true'.

would presumably have to be wider than purposes achievable solely within human existence: in *that* sense it would be 'ananthropocentric', to use Tim Mulgan's (2015) term. However, Mulgan's 'ananthropcentric purposivism' leaves it open that cosmic purposes have *nothing* to do with human existence. But that seems excluded if a metaphysics of cosmic purpose is to ground an account of ultimate reality that functions *religiously* to support not only moral ideals, but also the reasonable hope that humans may find ultimate fulfilment in pursuing them.[31] A viably *religious* 'purposivism' would have to posit some *disclosure* of humanity's place in the ultimate cosmic purpose. But that may (necessarily) be only a *limited* disclosure of what that ultimate purpose is – sufficient for the practical understanding humans need to contribute to, and participate in, its fulfilment. That disclosure, as already noted, cannot be made by scientific inquiry. Typically, religious traditions treat the purpose of human existence (or, at least, the practicalities of 'chiming' with that purpose) as something needing 'special' revelation that occurs in particular historical circumstances – for example, through human or angelic 'messengers'. The claimed revealed truths are then held to be accessible now only through authoritative traditions and writings – which need interpretation and are thus open to being contested. Prima facie, however, epistemologies of special revelation don't fit with worldviews that take science seriously, so, on the face of it, a 'purposivist' religious naturalism would need an alternative, naturalist, way of accessing that purpose and human ways of relating to it. (In Section 5 we'll discuss further how a religious naturalism might specify an overall cosmic purpose.)

An all-encompassing teleology has its appeal, yet naturalists may feel that this route to a more robustly religious perspective is beyond their reach because (or so they fear) it is bound to violate their essential one-world-ist stance. Loyal Rue (2004: 364f) captures this dilemma. In his view, a satisfying religious naturalism needs a 'root metaphor' that integrates evolutionary cosmology and eco-centric morality. However, as he says, 'the problem with specifying a root metaphor for religious naturalism has to do with specifying a goal or purpose (telos) for the natural order'. That notion seems just what is needed, yet (as Rue and others see it) naturalism rules it out. As Charley Hardwick (2003: 112) says of 'so-called' religious naturalists who posit cosmic teleology, they are 'nostalgically try[ing] to smuggle something from the theist tradition into the metaphysical basis for their

---

[31] This is not to deny that, as Mulgan (2015) argues, an ananthropocentric purposivism (AP) for which human life is irrelevant to cosmic purposes could yield moral ideals (see ch. 13 for Mulgan's discussion). On Mulgan's view, AP may admit God, though not the benevolent God of the theist traditions. In later work, Mulgan (2022) argues that AP *could* serve more robust religious functions, though his argument depends on accepting that human life can fulfil cosmic purposes only to a 'cosmically insignificant degree' (296) that 'makes no difference to whether or not this universe is valuable enough to exist' (Mulgan, personal communication).

religious affirmations ... giving up God but then trying to salvage teleology or final causality'. His implication is that no such salvage is possible.

These reservations, we suggest, take insufficient account of the religious naturalist potential of the idea of a cosmic purpose arising from the inherent directedness of reality upon a *telos* which is the good *for reality as such*, and thus the supreme good. We'll pursue that suggestion by discussing, in the next subsection, the prospects for a *euteleological religious naturalism*. In recent work (Bishop and Perszyk, 2023), we outlined and defended a one-world-ist metaphysics we call *euteleology*. We did so in the context of seeking an adequate alternative to the standard understanding of God as literally a personal being who is all-powerful, all-knowing, and perfectly good ('the personal omniGod'). But we granted that euteleology might provide sound foundations for other religious worldviews which do not use the concept of God. Euteleology is worth considering, then, as a foundational metaphysics for religious naturalism – especially since, as just noted, some religious naturalists identify a cosmic teleology as something they could do with but (probably) can't have.

4.3 Euteleological Religious Naturalism

Euteleology holds that reality *as such and as a whole* has a purpose which is the good for reality, and thus the supreme good ('*eu*' = well, good; '*telos*' = end, purpose). Furthermore, euteleology holds that the contingent Universe exists ultimately *because* it realizes reality's purpose – in the sense that the Universe contains states of affairs which fulfil that purpose (by realizing that end, or *telos*). For euteleology, the purposiveness of reality – its directedness on concretely realizing the supreme good – is *inherent*: there is directed*ness* upon an end, but no Direct*or* who produces the world for that end. Euteleology is thus explicitly one-world-ist, and its basic claims necessarily go beyond but not against a scientific understanding of reality. Its metaphysics thus qualify as potentially foundational for a religious perspective that is (expansively) naturalist.

Now, as our discussion of Aristotelian naturalism indicates, there's nothing incoherent about the idea of a naturally inherent purpose. Something's having a purpose is not conceptually restricted to the idea of its having been intelligently designed or produced to contribute to achieving a consciously chosen end.[32] Still,

---

[32] John Haught says this: 'In the broadest sense purpose means "directed toward a goal or *telos*".' (2006: 98). Later he adds: ' ... purpose [can] simply [mean] *the actualizing of value*. What makes any series of events purposive is that it is aiming toward, or actually bringing about, something ... *good*' (101). Anthony Kenny (2009: 118) writes: 'Design differs from purpose because design is purpose preceded by an idea: a thought, or blueprint, in somebody's mind', a remark which at least opens the conceptual space for the coherence of the notion of inherent purpose (i.e., without intelligent design aimed at achieving that purpose).

euteleology's prospects as a naturalist metaphysics need defence against the common objection that there can be no cosmic purpose without a supernatural Purposer. As directed against euteleology, that objection maintains that being real can't inherently involve directedness upon an ultimate *telos* (the supreme good), since there can be an ultimate *telos* only if there is a creator who creates everything real in order to contribute to achieving that end. In reply, we argue that the objection faces a version of Plato's famous '*Euthyphro*' question.[33] Does the Creator choose to create for a certain purpose because fulfilling that purpose is the supreme good for reality, or is reality's overall purpose and supreme good what it is just because the Creator chooses that purpose in creating? If you are a value realist – that is, you think that the supreme good is 'objectively' what it is – you will answer that it is the former: the Creator sees what the supreme good *is*, and creates a world in order to make that goodness concretely real. But in that case, the notion of what's inherently the good for reality is prior to, and presupposed by, the Creator's creatively acting to realize that good.

We conclude, then, that it is coherent to hold that reality is inherently purposive, and thus that the Universe has an inherent cosmic purpose, *provided that* value-realism is itself coherent. However, the insistence that there'd be no cosmic purpose without a supernatural Purposer remains unchallenged on an anti-realist ('subjectivist' or 'relativist') view which holds that values can exist only through valu*ings* by beings with minds. If there were a supernatural Intelligence, anti-realists will say, the cosmos could exist to realize an overall purpose; but the *Euthyphro*-type question would then get the opposing ('theistic subjectivist') answer that the cosmic purpose is the supreme good because it is the purpose the creating Intelligence ('God') chooses. Of course, naturalists rule out any such supernatural Being. But typically, as well, naturalists rule out a cosmic purpose, holding that the only purposes there can be in nature come onto the scene late in the evolutionary story. As Crosby (2007: 497) puts it, '*[p]urpose is an emergent phenomenon not a primordial one*'.[34]

---

[33] In this early Platonic dialogue, Socrates probes Euthyphro's understanding of the nature of piety, motivated by the confidence with which Euthyphro regards it as his pious duty to take his own father to court for allowing the death of a miscreant slave who had killed one of his fellows. When, in response to Socrates's questioning, Euthyphro suggests that the pious may be defined as whatever is pleasing to (all) the gods, Socrates asks him whether the gods love the pious because it is pious or the pious is pious because it is loved by the gods (*Euthyphro* 10a). Euthyphro replies that it is the former, and Socrates then pursues the question whether that reply can be consistent with Euthyphro's suggested definition.

[34] Crosby's own 'naturism', however, is committed to claims which might suggest a primordial cosmic purpose. Crosby (2002: 154) says that 'that which exists necessarily and thus never will cease to do so is the creative power (*natura naturans*) underlying and producing all of the systems of nature that ever have been or ever will be'. In his (2015), he speaks of 'primordial novelty', and, in his (2023), of the 'creative power of two primordial principles' (matter-energy and time). Thus, as Jeffrey Speaks (2024: 55) argues, what is metaphysically ultimate for Crosby

That stance overlooks the fact that, for an expansive one-world-ist naturalism that accepts value-realism, the notion of a primordial inherent purpose for reality itself *is* coherent. It might still be thought, though, that a 'eutelic' natural Universe couldn't exist without something to bring it into existence, and thus that appeal would still need to be made to supernatural agency. Naturalists therefore typically hold that the Universe, though containing purposes within it, exists overall as a matter of sheer brute contingency. The trouble is that viewing the Universe's existence as brutely contingent doesn't sit easily with being religious. Accepting brute contingency at the ontological foundations clashes with religiously realist perspectives which hold the Universe to be valuable and 'meaningful' *in itself*, not merely as conferred by human imagination. These 'thicker' religious perspectives thus take it that, though the Universe's existence is contingent, it is not a *sheer brute* contingency because there is an *ultimate* explanation for the contingent existence of anything at all (rather than nothing), and, indeed, for the existence of a Universe of the kind that we experience it as being.

But how could such ultimate explanations for contingent existence be possible? Many naturalist philosophers would dismiss them out of hand. *Ultimate* explanation is impossible, they would claim, because explanations have to stop with something that remains, at least for the time being, unexplained. That is entirely true for ordinary causal explanations. But religious explanations that posit an *ultimate and overall* meaningfulness for existence cannot be satisfied with resting on brute contingencies: they need to rest, somehow, on 'how things have to be', and not just on 'how things are'. Religious ultimate explanations of existence, then, cannot be ordinary causal explanations. Ultimate explanations must rely on positing some transcendent form of causation which can apply to the unique case of the whole of contingent reality.

To give content to an ultimate explanation, then, one must rely on some *analogous extension* from some mundane ways of understanding why something exists. Consider, for example, the *theological* ultimate explanation in the Abrahamic traditions, explaining the Universe as a creation by a creator whose existence is necessary. Since, on this account, the Universe does not arise from any pre-existent ordered material, ultimately explaining it as a creation involves analogous extension from our ordinary understanding of an agent's intentionally producing something from something else within the mundane causal order. The intelligibility of this theological ultimate explanation rests wholly on the force of analogy, and, for that very reason, cannot be made theoretically precise. No one could fully comprehend

---

is not simply Nature, but Nature as *natura naturans* – as exercising dynamic creative powers. Could Nature have such dynamic creative powers without their being inherently directed towards some overall purpose? Perhaps so, but in that case those natural powers would arguably be 'creative' only in an attenuated sense.

how the causation posited by an ultimate explanation such as this actually 'works' (such explanations are thus, in that sense, 'incomprehensible').

What kind of ultimate explanation could a – suitably expansive – naturalist perspective admit? The case can be made that the euteleological explanation that the Universe exists 'because it does what it's for' provides a religious naturalist ultimate explanation for existence. 'The Universe exists because it fulfils the purpose of its existence', or 'because it realizes its own telic good' (which is equivalent), is not an ordinary causal explanation. If it were, it would effectively be saying, absurdly, that the Universe pulls itself into existence by its own bootstraps. But this euteleological explanation is an *ultimate* explanation, positing a transcendent form of causation whose 'workings' can't be grasped and which is intelligible only *by analogy with* some familiar form of explanation. And we do sometimes explain why something exists in terms of its 'doing what it's for'. Tools and artefacts exist because they serve their ends, and the same applies to biological functions – for example, hearts have the function of pumping blood, and exist because this is the function for which they were selected through processes of natural selection. Of course, in cases like these 'it exists because it does what it's for' is *only part* of the full explanation: some process (involving intelligent action in the case of tools and artefacts, though not in the case of functioning animal organs) has to bring about the thing's existence. Still, if you didn't recognize that the thing fulfils its purpose, your understanding, not merely of what it is, but also of why it exists, would be incomplete. Certainly, recognizing that something is achieving its purpose is enough to assure you that it doesn't 'just happen' to exist. That kind of (partial) explanation of something's existence provides the basis, then, for thinking, *by an analogous extension*, of the entire Universe as existing ultimately *only* because it fulfils its purpose.

Ultimate explanations for existence should not, we think, be regarded as produced by theoretical reasoning (through a supposed metaphysical 'higher science'). Rather, they should be regarded as posits recommended for acceptance in the context of our practical reasonings about how to live well in the world. (We echo here a key theme from Immanuel Kant's critical philosophy.) That practical and ethical context is where religion operates. Religious worldviews offer an overall stance on the kind of reality in which we find ourselves – on questions about what really matters, what we may hope for, and what makes those hopes reasonable even when commitment to what really matters is fraught and costly. Satisfying answers to these questions seem to need ultimates posited as holding necessarily – foundational values, and a stance on ultimate reality that secures these values and makes it reasonable to pursue them in the hope of their fulfilment. Such a stance cannot leave it as brute that the Universe exists; there needs to be an ultimate explanation that 'makes sense of' contingent existence.

We think that euteleology includes transcendent features which yield these kinds of ultimates, yet without infringing a one-world-ist stance, since the transcendent features are not transcendent *beings*. The transcendent foundation of euteleological metaphysics is the necessity of reality's being inherently directed upon realizing its *telos*, the good for reality as such and as a whole, and thus the supreme good. The nature of this *telos* determines what really matters: the mind-independent values are what they are because reality is what it is, namely inherently directed upon its telic good.[35] Euteleology's ultimate explanation for the Universe's existence – namely, that the Universe realizes the purpose for which it exists – implies that reality's telic good is actually contingently realized within the Universe. In turn, this implies the existence of powers able to realize reality's *telos*, powers which are within the natural world: whatever their religious characterization, they operate consistently with natural powers as known to science.

Euteleological metaphysics, then, has the potential to support an expansive naturalism with religious hope-grounding, broadly soteriological, functions.[36] Our description of a euteleological religious naturalism remains schematic, however, until something substantive is said about what reality's *telos* is – a topic we take up in Section 5.

4.4 Comparing Alternatives

In this final subsection on religious naturalism and cosmic purpose, we'll consider alternatives to the euteleological approach just sketched. As we've seen, there can be 'thinner' forms of religious naturalism that keep to the constraints of metaphysical scientific naturalism. Some religious naturalists expand their naturalism to include value-realism, but proceed no further. But for those who expand their metaphysics to provide grounds in ultimate reality not only for real values but also for the hopeful pursuit of those values, what alternative is there to the euteleological approach?

John Schellenberg deals with notions of transcendence and ultimacy in the context of advocating 'evolutionary religion'. Schellenberg holds that, for all we

---

[35] Euteleology may therefore seem to provide more depth to value realism than a purely Platonic metaphysics that posits the mind-independent necessary existence of the Form of the Good. However, defenders of 'attributivism' about the meaning of 'good' – namely, that what's good is always what's good *for* some specific kind of thing – may presumably argue that Plato's Form of the Good must be understood as the Form of the Good *for reality as such*, and, if that's the case, euteleology has Platonic foundations. (For a recent discussion of attributivism about the good, see Richard Kraut 2011, ch. 30.)

[36] These are the functions we discussed above, in Section 2.3. A full understanding of these functions of a robust religious perspective requires understanding the relevant concept of hope. For a discussion of the kind of 'living in hope' that may be grounded in a euteleological religious naturalism, see Georg Gasser (2025), and our response to him, Bishop and Perszyk (2025b).

know, humanity is only at a very early stage of religious consciousness, so that there is enormous potential for religious development.[37] As noted earlier (Section 2.2, note 6), Schellenberg characterizes religious development as involving beliefs about metaphysical, axiological, and soteriological transcendence, and he describes as 'ultimist' belief-systems which posit something transcendent in all three of these respects. Could there be an ultimist religious naturalism? Well, not if (as Schellenberg often seems to imply) ultimism requires the necessary existence of a triply transcendent *being* (since such an entity would be supernatural and so infringe one-world-ism). But if a perspective can be ultimist by having suitably integrated metaphysical, axiological, and soteriological ultimates that do not imply the existence of any concrete entities beyond the natural world, then euteleology is just such an ultimist naturalism – assuming, that is, that euteleology's basic metaphysics can be filled out in a religiously satisfactory way, which is our topic for Section 5.[38]

Pantheism may be thought to offer obvious prospects for a robust religious naturalism. But how does pantheism relate to euteleological metaphysics? A religiously viable pantheism regards the whole of reality not simply as a sum total or collection of things but as a unified whole.[39] Now, reality can be a unified whole only if there is some principle of unity that integrates its vast diversity. What could that unifying principle be other than the directedness of everything real upon an overall, ultimate, *telos* as posited by euteleology? There may be other possibilities: perhaps the unifying principle could be purely aesthetic, or perhaps the principle could be the 'genealogical' relatedness of everything with everything else (as implied, for example, by the centrality of *whakapapa* in the Māori worldview – to be discussed further in Section 5.2). But, in any case, it is clear that a eutelic Universe *would be* a unified whole in virtue of its having and realizing an overall purpose; and it is therefore justifiable to regard a pantheist option as amongst the possible ways of developing euteleological religious naturalism. Obviously, pantheism will appeal specifically only when significance is attached to using a concept of God: we'll return to consider options such as Spinoza's *Deus sive Natura* in a wider discussion of religious naturalisms that are in some way theistic (Section 5.3). In that context, too, we'll consider panentheist options – according to which the world is somehow 'in' God, though God is 'more than' the world – given that some panentheisms can be understood in a one-world-ist naturalist way.

Panpsychism – roughly, the thesis that consciousness is a fundamental and ubiquitous feature of reality – has recently attracted attention in analytic philosophy

---

[37] See, e.g., Schellenberg (2013).

[38] For further discussion of the relationship between euteleology and ultimism, see Bishop and Perszyk (forthcoming).

[39] We have already remarked on this essential feature of religious pantheism (see note 12).

of mind.⁴⁰ Some may urge that euteleology must itself be panpsychist because they think that reality's being inherently directed upon the realization of the good requires that everything real must be, in some rudimentary sense, 'minded'. But we remain unpersuaded, since it seems to us that there is no a priori reason to exclude the possibility that matter may exhibit reality's inherent directedness upon the good.

But there are many varieties of panpsychism which develop the idea beyond the claim that everything is conscious in some rudimentary sense: could any of these provide an alternative to a euteleological religious naturalism? Philip Goff (2023: 131) favours a form of panpsychism in which the Universe itself is conscious 'as something that recognizes and responds to considerations of value'. He adds: 'On the view we can call "teleological cosmopsychism", the Universe is essentially driven to try to maximize the good.' Goff offers this proposal as his preferred explanation for there being a cosmic purpose, faith in which serves religious functions. In its content, then, Goff's account seems similar to euteleology, though Goff goes further in the direction of a theoretical explanation for cosmic purpose. He thinks that his teleological cosmopsychism best explains the fine-tuning of the fundamental physical constants for the emergence of life by hypothesizing that 'the Universe fine-tuned itself' (132).⁴¹

Eric Steinhart (2023) has proposed an 'atheistic Platonist' religious naturalism that is also similar to euteleology.⁴² His proposal supports objective values and posits an overall purpose for the Universe, which Steinhart takes to be a multiverse. But, by contrast with Goff, Steinhart (2023: 15) takes ultimate reality to be mindless and denies that purpose requires an intelligent purpose-giver. Far from

---

⁴⁰ See, e.g., Godehard Brüntrup and Ludwig Jaskolla (2017). For a comprehensive, (Western) historical study of panpsychism, see David Skrbina (2017).

⁴¹ Goff (2023: 132) says he needs to add a further postulation, namely, the following:

> If, during the first split second of time, the Universe fine-tuned itself in order to allow for the emergence of life billions of years in the future, the Universe must in some sense have been aware of this future possibility, in order to act in such a way as to bring it about. To account for this, we can attribute to the Universe conscious awareness of the full possible consequences of each of the options available to it.

Furthermore, Goff identifies 'the cosmic-fine tuner' with 'the wave function itself'. He explains that '[o]n the resulting view the wave-function is a conscious entity that is aware of the complete future consequences of the options available to it and acts by choosing the best one' (136). This claim looks like a variant of 'Molinism', but with the universal wave-function taking the place of God. According to (standard) Molinism – named after the sixteenth-century Spanish Jesuit Luis de Molina – 'prior' to creation God knows what would result from every possible creative option open to 'him'. The suggestion that a wave-function could be conscious seems to us to involve a category-error – though on matters quantum mechanical we lack confidence in applying ordinary intuitions.

⁴² Steinhart himself (2023: 31) acknowledges this similarity, saying that 'the euteleology of Bishop and Perszyk (2017) looks like a kind of Christian Platonism. It has many structural affinities with atheistic Platonism'.

being a conscious mind that fine-tunes itself, the Universe's fine-tuning results, according to Steinhart's Platonism, from 'a mindless cosmic optimization algorithm'. This 'atheoplatonist' ultimate explanation for existence is an extreme axiarchic one, as in the theories of John Leslie (1979) and Nicholas Rescher (1984), who hold that its goodness alone is what ultimately explains why anything exists. Thus, Steinhart (2023: 17) says, the 'abstract laws of value-maximization (that is axiological laws) entail the existence of concrete things'.

Euteleology also seems similar to Thomas Nagel's (2012) proposal for 'a naturalistic teleology'. Nagel suggests that in addition to physical laws of the familiar kind there are underlying natural teleological laws directed upon the emergence of life. Teleology would then inform the Universe's development throughout its evolution, rather than being a purely emergent feature, as Crosby (2015: 101), responding to Nagel, claims it must be. Nagel's proposal looks more straightforward than the theoretical speculations about naturalist cosmic purpose made by either Goff or Steinhart.[43] Euteleology, too, need not make any such theoretical speculations – it simply posits that the Universe has, and realizes, an overall *telos* that is the good for reality as such, and is, therefore, the supreme good. Unlike Nagel, euteleology explicitly offers a one-world naturalist *religious metaphysics*. As we said in Section 4.3, we think of metaphysics in a Kantian way, not as arrived at by theoretical reasoning, but rather as making posits about ultimate reality that can be recommended for acceptance as an overall practical orientation in our seeking to live well in the world. A euteleological stance on reality is thus viable provided that all we know about the Universe (in our necessarily limited way) can coherently be interpreted in terms of the Universe's having, and realizing, an ultimate purpose which is inherent in reality as such. Euteleology's metaphysical posits must thus be consistent with, though they necessarily go beyond, our best empirical scientific understanding of the world. Whether a euteleological religious perspective is viable will require some specification of reality's inherent purpose, or, at least, what it implies for human existence – an issue we'll turn to in Section 5. Our point now is that euteleology, as a foundation for a religious naturalism, can remain content with our best scientific cosmological theories *as they stand* (noting that whatever specification is given of reality's *telos* and its implications will have

---

[43] Nagel (2012: 93) sees his naturalistic teleology as a middle path between what he takes to be Darwinian naturalism/materialism and Intelligent Design. He says: 'naturalistic teleology would mean that organizational and developmental principles ... are an irreducible part of the natural order, and not the result of intentional or purposive influence by anyone. I am not confident that this Aristotelian idea of teleology without intention makes sense, but I do not at the moment see why it doesn't.'

Goff (2023: ch. 5) discusses Nagel's proposal and suggests that teleological laws might have 'done their work' in the Plank epoch (shortly – very shortly! – after the Big Bang) by effectively selecting the fundamental physical constants in the narrow range needed for it to be possible for life to emerge.

to be consistent with these theories). Euteleology has no need to engage in theoretical cosmological speculations, as Nagel, Goff, and Steinhart do, about how it could actually 'work' that the cosmos has a purpose without a Purposer. These views give hostage to fortune by resting a naturalist view of cosmic purpose on speculative cosmological hypotheses. Euteleology avoids that trap.

A further distinguishing feature of euteleology emerges from comparing it with theories such as Goff's and Steinhart's which seem to seek something within the natural world which plays the same role as an Intelligent Designer – in particular, by selecting the values of the fundamental physical constants within the (very) narrow range needed for conscious life to be possible within the Universe. These theories, though naturalist, thus effectively remain within the 'deist' Enlightenment paradigm of a purposive Universe having to arise from an initial agent or agency that 'sets it up' so as to realize its given purpose. Euteleology, by contrast, takes everything that exists as inherently directed upon the supreme good as its purpose, and existing – ultimately – only because that purpose is actually realized in concrete existence. This may be viewed as a 'naturalization' of the classical theist paradigm in which everything that exists in the Universe does so only through God's action, not merely in initiating, but also sustaining its existence. This is a 'naturalization' in the sense that euteleology has no being or entity in its fundamental ontology that can be identified with God. As we've noted, we hold the (controversial) view that euteleology (despite holding that God is 'no-thing') is an apt metaphysics for Abrahamic theism. That view fits with the idea that classical theism is – surprisingly to many analytic philosophers – *itself* a religious naturalism (a point we'll return to in discussing theist naturalisms in Section 5.3).

Our discussion of naturalist theories of cosmic purpose in general has been brief. But we hope to have said enough to conclude that there is good reason to pursue the possibility of a robust religious naturalism by understanding it as having euteleological foundations. Our next step is to consider how one might build on those foundations.

5 Resources for a Robust Religious Naturalism

How may we further specify a robustly religious naturalist worldview that posits an overall purpose for the Universe? Naturalist theories of cosmic purpose are usually offered against background assumptions about what that purpose is – the emergence of conscious life, for example. But these theories don't *by themselves* settle that question. For all we know, that purpose might be something prior in cosmic evolution to the emergence of life. Perhaps, for example, the Universe's purpose is to generate supernovae explosions, with life simply a by-product. It's also left open that the purpose may be wholly anthropocentric in a way that wouldn't support the kind of eco-morality which religious naturalisms typically advocate. The same general point may be made about euteleology: positing that reality has an inherent purpose and the Universe wouldn't exist if it didn't realize that supreme good doesn't guarantee that the purpose is the kind that would support a religious naturalism that brings the whole of nature within the scope of its concern. How, then, may a purpose of that kind be specified?

5.1 A Naturalist Conception of an 'Integrative' Supreme Good

Any naturalist account of the overall purpose and supreme good will have to hold that it may be realized within the one, natural, world. This contrasts with religious perspectives that locate the fulfilment of reality's purpose in a guaranteed final consummation in which the natural, historical, order passes away, and perfect goodness is achieved incorruptibly in a supra-natural eternal order of existence. Naturalists reject any such picture, even if, in the style of Hegel (2019 [1807]) or Teilhard de Chardin (1999), eternal perfection is understood as emerging as the necessitated ultimate stage of the Universe's development. The natural Universe evolves and develops, and may be more fundamentally 'process' than 'substance', but, on a one-world naturalist view, it does not evolve inevitably into an incorruptible final stage. Euteleological religious naturalism understands the fulfilment of reality's inherent purpose as obtaining, not in some trans-historical eschaton, but in certain kinds of natural conditions. The fulfilment of reality's *telos* is thus in *multiple* manifestations or realizations of that supreme good. Those realizations are contingent – they come about and they pass away – though the supreme good itself is transcendent over ('more than') its actual realizations.[44] And there's no basis for limiting how many such realizations there may be.[45]

But what are those natural conditions which fulfil the Universe's overall purpose? For euteleology to support a religious perspective that grounds an adequate environmental ethics, they must be conditions which realize the values underlying that kind of eco-morality. These values may be characterized

---

[44] The transcendence of the supreme good rests on reality's being inherently eutelic, which (if it is a truth) is a necessary truth. Could it be argued, then, that euteleology is, after all, committed to a supra-natural 'realm' inhabited by *that which makes it true* that being real is being real for the sake of realizing a specific *telos*, which is the supreme good? Clearly that truth is not made true by anything belonging to the Universe of contingent entities, processes, and states of affairs. But neither is it made true by any concretely and necessarily existing being 'outside' the natural Universe. Whatever makes it true, then, seems to have the same kind of status as Plato's intelligible universal Forms, which he held to be 'beyond existence' (see, e.g., *Republic*, Book 6).

[45] Euteleology leaves it open that the Universe (= all that contingently exists) may be a 'multiverse' – that is, it may consist in a, possibly infinite, multiplicity of distinct spatio-temporal small-u universes, of which our own Big-Bang-initiated cosmos is but one.

broadly as the *flourishing* of natural ecosystems, of humans and other living species, and of the wider physical environment. If the Universe's realizing its overall purpose is achieved in such flourishing, it seems to follow that, whatever it is in itself, the supreme good (the good for reality as such) should be understood as an essentially integrating or *integrative* good – as we'll now explain.

Euteleology's basic axiom is that *everything* real is 'eutelic': everything real inherently exists for the sake of realizing the good for reality as such, the supreme good. Whatever that supreme good is, it must be something to whose realization every kind of thing, functioning as it should, can contribute in the ways characteristic of its kind. This integrating function of the supreme good fits well with the idea that the supreme good is *itself* an integrative good, rather than a single uniform good hierarchically elevated over other goods. The good for reality as such and as a whole would then amount to the goodness of *a way or ways of relating and/or being related* that makes room for a wide diversity of different goods while unifying them within an overall harmony. The practical and ethical salience of such an integrative supreme good would then depend on human understanding *of what that integrative mode of relating is like in human lived experience*, and how, in practice, it brings into a proper balance sometimes competing concerns for the many different goods that humans can recognize as goods for themselves, for other species, for ecosystems, and for the Earth itself. Indeed, it may be beyond human mastery to understand theoretically the essential nature of the supreme good (it may, in just that sense, be 'incomprehensible'): instead, our limited and open-endedly developing understanding of what the supreme good is may depend on what we take to be paradigm examples of its manifestation in human experience.

What more may we say – even in a limited and open-ended way – about what this integrative, relational, supreme good could be? As noted earlier (Section 2.4), religious naturalists may find it useful to draw for content on existing religious and cultural traditions. Perhaps existing traditions can throw light on the nature and practical implications of the supreme good a euteleological naturalism may posit. In any case, we'll now turn to a discussion of how much help existing traditions may be in providing resources for a viably functioning robust religious naturalism. We'll begin (in Section 5.2) by discussing resources that may be drawn from pagan and Indigenous worldviews which seem to be both one-worldist and affirming of nature-friendly values.

5.2 Lessons from Indigenous Worldviews

It's not surprising that 'Western' thinkers drawn to the idea that the natural world is sacred should be attracted to pagan worldviews displaced in Europe by

Christianity, but existing still in revived contemporary forms, such as Wicca.[46] Similarly attractive are the Indigenous worldviews of peoples colonized by European powers – worldviews now treated with respect by those committed to an intellectual 'decolonisation' which seeks so far as it can to abandon deep assumptions about the superiority of the colonisers' cultures over those of the Indigenous peoples. These Indigenous and pagan worldviews typically treat human existence as highly integrated with the natural world.[47]

Since Aotearoa/New Zealand is our home, we'll take *te ao Māori* (the Māori worldview) as an example, relying on sources from those who have standing within Māori culture.[48] In *te ao Māori*, human *whakapapa* (genealogy) and indeed the *whakapapa* of all creatures traces back to the Earth Mother (*Papatūānuku*) and the Sky Father (*Ranginui*) themselves. There are higher powers, *atua*, the children of *Papatūānuku* and *Ranginui*, of whom *Tāne* (god of forests and birds) took the lead in prising his parents apart to create the space where creatures may dwell. All beings, including higher powers and energies on which human life depends, are thus interrelated.[49] This integrated understanding of human life within the natural world supports the kinds of values of conservation and sustainability that religious naturalism will typically seek to affirm. It's true that a well-known Māori *whakatauki* (proverb) emphasizes the importance of humanity.[50] But the integration of humanity with the wider natural world entails that there can be no deep

---

[46] See, e.g., Starhawk (1999) for a distinctive Wiccan perspective. John Beckett (2017), who is a Druid, offers a more general introduction to modern pagan beliefs and practices. For a wide-ranging overview of the history and recent development of pagan views, see Murphy Pizza and James Lewis's (2009) collection of essays. Also see Steinhart (2017), who discusses both old and new pagan 'energy' religions. He focuses on four (non-theistic) energy religions that are naturalistic: religions of conscience (e.g., New Stoicism and Westernized Buddhism), religions of vision (that use entheogens – psychoactive substances that induce visionary experiences), religions of dance (e.g., raves), and religions of beauty (e.g., Burning Man). See Steinhart (2025a) for his most recent discussion of contemporary pagan philosophy.

[47] 'New Animists' take to heart the ways that Indigenous peoples interact with plants, animals, and things typically treated by Westerners as inanimate (e.g., rivers and mountains). For a range of Native American Indian examples and stories, which challenge or blur the distinction between persons and non-persons, see, e.g., Robin Wall Kimmerer (2013). For an introduction to New Animism, see Graham Harvey (2005).

[48] We are both Pākehā, of British and American/Polish-German ancestry respectively, so have no standing ourselves to articulate a Māori worldview. Māori views of the world have been passed on through oral tradition, and the narratives that express it vary from one *iwi* (tribe) to another, so talk of 'the' Māori worldview should be treated cautiously.

[49] See, e.g., Natasha Tassell-Matamua et al. (2023), Gareth Harmsworth and Shaun Awatere (2013), and Mere Roberts (2012). For a more detailed and nuanced synopsis of Māori cosmological narratives (creation stories), see, e.g., Tassell-Matamua et al. (2021: 83–5).

[50] *He aha te mea nui o te ao? He tāngata he tāngata he tāngata!* (What is the most important thing in the world? It is people, it is people, it is people!) It might be inferred that the values of deep ecology are not found in *te ao Māori*. But it is probably more accurate to say that the question simply doesn't arise whether, as deep ecologists maintain, value could belong to ecosystems

conflict between caring for people and caring for the natural environment – after all, people are part of that environment, and have *whanaunatanga* (kinship) with all that dwells within it. Māori thus affirm the values of *kaitiakitanga* (guardianship), with *tangata whenua* (people of the land) having the authority to exercise that guardianship over the environment in the area to which they are ancestrally related.

It doesn't follow, of course, that *te ao Māori* is itself a religious naturalism. It is culturally inept to 'read into' the Māori worldview anything religious in the common 'Western' sense of a specific 'department' of human life, to be distinguished from 'the secular' or 'the scientific'.[51] Nevertheless, the holistic character of *te ao Māori* does fulfil a characteristically religious function in providing a practically salient overall interpretation or framework for human life in the world.

From a Western perspective, Māori ritual behaviours that relate to the *atua* such as *karakia* (translated as 'prayers') and the rituals relating to *tapu* and the lifting of *tapu*, will tend to get classified as religious and be regarded as implying belief in 'the supernatural'. Similarly, Māori writers often speak of physical and spiritual 'realms' or 'worlds', and this might easily be taken to imply a commitment to two-world-ism. But the highly integrated perspective on reality found in *te ao Māori* and widely characteristic of Indigenous worldviews generally is not consistent with accepting an order of concrete existence that is radically distinct from the natural order.[52] *Te ao Māori* is – in the terminology we've been using – one-world-ist. True, it involves 'belief in' spiritual forces and higher powers or energies, but these belong *within* the one integrated reality to which human life and experience belongs. Thus, *mauri* (life force, energy) is 'the bonding element that knits all the diverse elements within the Universal "Procession" giving creation its unity in diversity' (Māori Marsden, 2003: 44). The *atua* might be said to be 'supernatural' in the sense that they are beings or energetic forces greater than, or 'above', humans and other animals; but they are definitely not *supra*-natural in the sense that they belong to a distinct ontological order 'beyond' nature (as a personal deity whose agency produces the entire natural order would do).[53] Similarly, Māori beliefs

---

quite independently of humanity's relation to them. Such speculations have little salience given the practical focus of Indigenous worldviews.

[51] A similar point applies in the context of Native American Indians. See, e.g., Vine Deloria (2003: 151f).

[52] On the rejection of two-world-ism in the case of Native American Indians, see, e.g., Deloria (1999, e.g., chapters 4 and 28) and Thomas Norton-Smith (2018: 226f).

[53] For more details on the deep connection between Māori identity and the environment, and how it undercuts the distinction between the natural and supernatural, see, e.g., Christopher Lockhart et al. (2019, especially section 1).

There has been recent philosophical discussion about the (ontological) status of *taniwha* – often depicted as serpent- or dragon-like beings, dwelling usually in specific places in the ocean,

about their *tīpuna* (ancestors) don't invoke a radically separate supra-natural order. According to some Māori traditions, the *wairua* (spirits) of the dead dwell in Hawaiki, and they voyage to it in a *waka* (canoe) from a specific place of departure (Spirits Bay), and so return to the place from which Māori are held to have sailed to New Zealand. There's not so much a blurring of spiritual or mythical and physical or geographical reality here, as, from this Māori perspective, a stance towards reality for which such distinctions are not fundamental.

Religious naturalists may identify in an Indigenous worldview such as *te ao Māori* not only nature-friendly values but also the kind of integrated one-world expansive naturalist stance that they seek to affirm. Indigenous worldviews themselves do not, however, seem to use the idea of a cosmic purpose, or the euteleological notion of a supreme good whose realization in the world ultimately explains existence. Indigenous worldviews seem not to deal in ultimates, at least not explicitly. There is a Māori tradition of a supreme reality, *Io* – though it is controversial whether this tradition may reflect an incorporation of Christian missionary ideas rather than something authentically Polynesian.[54] Nevertheless, we think that euteleological religious naturalists may find encouragement in Indigenous worldviews such as *te ao Māori* for the idea that the supreme good which these religious naturalists posit is essentially an integrative good – an overall harmony of beings in the one natural world, into which humanity can fit, when we live wisely and well.

Finding encouragement for the idea of an integrative supreme good is different, of course, from actually attributing that concept to an Indigenous worldview – a further step requiring considerable caution. Analytical philosophers who deploy their own theoretical concepts in analyzing Indigenous worldviews can understandably be received (though perhaps often mistakenly) as assuming that Indigenous perspectives are 'valid' only when shown to be 'essentially' equivalent to, or indicative of, some 'developed' 'Western' view.[55] No such assumption of the intrinsic superiority or centrality of any one historical/cultural

---

waterways or caves, serving as *kaitiaki* (guardians), powerful and potentially dangerous. See Justine Kingsbury (2022) and subsequent critical commentaries by Heather Dyke (2023), Carl Mika (2023), and Krushil Watene (2023). Different *iwi* (tribes) have varied traditions about *taniwha*. But it's clear that, though *taniwha* may aptly enough be described as supernatural, they are part of the natural environment (not intervening agents from some supra-natural realm).

[54] For one detailed examination of both sides of this controversy, see James Cox (2014).

[55] A recent case in point involved Joanna Leidenhag's (2021) dismissal of animism in favour of panpsychism. Eugene Fuimaono (McKirkland and Fuimaono, 2024) thinks panpsychism isn't 'wholly transferable into Indigenous thought', but admits 'points of congruency with Māori theology'. While he doesn't think that Leidenhag herself is doing this, he reminds us that 'animism' has often been used as a catch-word in quick dismissals of Indigenous spiritualities. To avoid this trap, he thinks Leidenhag should look more closely at animism and the Indigenous views often associated with it. She may thereby achieve a deeper understanding of Indigenous ways of thinking and see no need to replace animism. In her response, Leidenhag (2024: 499)

intellectual tradition can be warranted if philosophy is to belong, as it surely does, to humankind as a whole. Philosophers must be able to engage in conversations aimed at satisfying a shared love of wisdom while properly respecting the limitations of their own historical/cultural situation and the plurality of ways in which human cultures have cognitively and intellectually framed human experience of reality and human life in the world. We dare to believe that this can be done – though no philosopher will find it easy to overcome hidden prejudices and avoid stereotypical over-simplifications, especially of traditions that are, consciously or unconsciously, being treated as 'other'. Comparisons of concepts as between different worldviews – especially when there's a history of colonialist oppression and power imbalances – thus need to be considered sensitively. To rule them altogether out of order, though, would be a mistake, apart from anything else because it would preclude the contribution concepts from Indigenous worldviews may make to wider philosophical understanding. Thus – to return to the specific question at issue – we're prepared to suggest that the concept of a cosmic purpose which is an overall integrative good *is* implicit in *te ao Māori*.[56] But we make that suggestion as (sympathetic) outsiders; on the question whether this suggestion could be accepted as authentic to *te ao Māori*, we defer to those with an insider's standing in *mātauranga Māori* (Māori knowledge).

Indigenous worldviews are naturalist in the one-world-ist sense, but some may question whether they take science seriously – something a robust religious naturalism needs to do. We think that considering an Indigenous worldview such as *te ao Māori* throws light on the wider context of this constraint. The root of this requirement is that our metaphysical religious posits should cohere with our best *experientially-based* understanding of our world. In an integrated worldview such as found in *te ao Māori* or in Native American worldviews, purely factual empirical knowledge isn't consciously separated out from experientially-based knowledge generally: experiential knowledge is essentially relational – concerned with how things are *and how things should be* related, and thus essentially focused on how humans should live in the world and relate rightly to all else that exists. Knowledge of facts and values are not conceived as categorially separate departments of knowledge, as in analytical philosophy.[57] As we have emphasized,

---

'repents' for implicitly (though unintentionally) perpetuating the marginalization or off-the-cuff dismissals of Indigenous knowledge and people.

[56] The same may apply to Native American Indian traditions. See, e.g., Thomas Norton-Smith's (2018: 226–27) discussion of the Native American response (given by Deloria) to the common 'Western' assumption (which some religious naturalists such as Crosby, Rue, and Corrington share) that a 'scientific' worldview must exclude the idea that nature has an overall purpose.

[57] It remains an important logical principle ('Hume's Law') that purely descriptive premises cannot entail normative propositions (for a recent defence, see Gillian Russell, 2023). Yet the integration

contemporary religious naturalists (of the more robustly religious kind) want a perspective that 'fits' with, though it necessarily goes beyond, a ('Western', empirical) scientific understanding of the world. Thus, their desire to integrate religion with science is matched with an equal desire to reintegrate science with religion. Robustly religious naturalists, that is, think that a 'non-religious' scientific worldview (the worldview of the metaphysical scientific naturalist) is inadequate. Indigenous worldviews, we are suggesting, hold out the prospect that such a re-integration is possible – and it does indeed count as *re*-integration to the extent that one has the sense (as many 'Westerners' do) that, in encountering Indigenous worldviews, we are making contact again with something very similar to our own ancestral understandings of the world.

5.3 Religious Naturalisms and Existing Religious Traditions

It is a common objection to the practical viability of a religious naturalism that it lacks communal institutions, practices, and rituals. Yet, as Crosby (2002: 156) points out, 'There is already a fertile field of potential materials – ideas, values, precepts, stories, myths, symbols, rituals, and the like – in existing religious traditions from which a religion of nature can draw in developing beliefs, evocations, objectives, and practices appropriate to itself'. In the previous subsection, we argued that attention to Indigenous worldviews may support a robustly religious naturalism that posits an integrative supreme good as the ultimate *telos* for the sake of which everything exists. In this subsection, we'll consider how existing religious traditions may supply content for a euteleological religious naturalism's understanding of the supreme good and what it is, in practice, to live with the faith that reality is inherently directed upon realizing that supreme good.

The question of how religious naturalisms may enhance their viability by drawing on existing religious traditions is a large topic which could not be tackled in general. Rather, those with an insider's understanding of Buddhism, Taoism, Hinduism, and so on, might consider what resources from their own traditions may support a religious naturalism (and, in particular, one based on the idea of reality's inherent purposiveness).[58] Those interested in religious pluralism might be motivated to consider whether the idea of an overall purpose

---

of facts and values characteristic of Indigenous worldviews alerts us to the importance of locating the practice and technical application of empirical science (itself properly driven by purely epistemic values) within a commitment to wider, ethical, values.

[58] The 2018 *Routledge Handbook of Religious Naturalism*, part V, edited by Crosby and Stone, has papers relating naturalism to Buddhism, Confucianism, Daoism, Hinduism, and Shawnee religion, in addition to Christianity and Judaism, though none say anything explicitly about euteleology.

and supreme good inherent in ultimate reality is a trope expressed in different ways in different religious traditions. On the face of it – from our own Judaeo-Christian influenced perspective – 'non-Western' religions do not explicitly use the idea of a supreme good which it is the Universe's purpose to realize. But, as we've suggested for Indigenous worldviews, perhaps such an idea is implicit in some non-theist religions. Taoism, for example, seems explicitly one-world-ist, but not euteleological. Nevertheless, a euteleological interpretation might perhaps be placed on Taoism by taking the ultimate *telos* and supreme good to be just the very exercise of the Qi, constantly achieving and then disrupting the balance between Yin and Yang.[59] As we've said, there's a project about resonances with religious naturalisms (of various forms) for each existing religious tradition. In this subsection, we'll confine ourselves to remarks about religious naturalist potential within the Abrahamic theist traditions.[60]

That focus may initially seem unpromising, since religious naturalists usually eschew God-talk. As Charley Hardwick (2003: 116) remarks, 'having stated their naturalism, [religious naturalists often] think they must then reject their own religious traditions on the assumption that those traditions are essentially and necessarily anti-naturalist'. But this, as Hardwick says, tends to leave them with little to say religiously – and, he adds, it is not evident that the monotheist traditions really are as profoundly anti-naturalist as often assumed. Some religious naturalists do indeed deploy the concept of God, and some continue to see themselves, furthermore, as adherents to a theist tradition, finding that this is needed for a naturalism that isn't religiously too thin. Their 'theistic naturalism' may require understanding the theist traditions in revisionary and unorthodox ways (as it may appear to some of their fellow adherents, anyway). Still, religious naturalists of this ilk will often insist that their inherited theist tradition is *best* understood as a religious naturalism that promotes a general human duty to respect, care for, and restore nature as God's creation.

Our discussion of Indigenous worldviews made it clear that an integrated one-world-ist worldview can accommodate small-g gods. Humans and higher ('supernatural') beings can belong together within the one world 'system'. But can the Abrahamic God also belong within that one system: can there be a (one-world-ist) naturalist conception of God? Not if the Abrahamic God must be literally understood as a personal being who is creator of all else that exists. Such a being would be an uncreated, supra-natural, being belonging to an ontological category distinct from the natural, created, world. That's how, on

---

[59] For a preliminary attempt at how a proposal of this kind might work from a Confucian and Taoist perspective, see, e.g., JeeLoo Liu (2014).

[60] Those with a particular interest in contemporary Christian naturalism should see Mikael Leidenhag (2024).

this picture, God's transcendence is understood: God's immanence within creation typically gets cashed out in terms of God's knowledge of and power over created beings. The God-world 'relation' is thus rather one-sided, and divine agency includes 'special divine acts' (miraculous interventions) in the natural world – something that doesn't sit well with religious naturalists who 'take science seriously'.

But this 'personalist' conception of God and of the God-world relation may be contested from within Abrahamic theist traditions. There are interpretations of theism as offering a religious expansive naturalism. For example, Spinoza's *Deus sive Natura* (God or Nature) rejects a supra-natural understanding of God's being, situating divine agency wholly within the natural world.[61] Spinoza has standardly been interpreted as a 'pantheist' (i.e., as identifying God with the world). Whether or not this is the best understanding of Spinoza's conception of God,[62] pantheism has certainly been an option for some. There are different sorts of pantheism.[63] Demian Wheeler (2018) argues that there are naturalistic versions of it. He discusses three examples: Spinoza, Loomer, and Corrington, before recommending his own 'apophatic pantheism'. These versions are all one-world-ist naturalisms, but it is doubtful whether they can sustain the more robust religious functions. Unsurprisingly, pantheism has no difficulty with divine immanence, but divine transcendence seems to disappear from the picture.[64]

Theological innovation in the twentieth century has yielded some understandings of Abrahamic theism which may sustain interpreting it as an expansive one-world-ist naturalism. Whitehead's process metaphysics has inspired process theologies, which typically understand God as co-evolving with the creation, in a give-and-take relationship with creatures. God's power is not all-controlling but is rather the power of love which 'lures' and empowers rather than dominates.[65] Process theologians often identify their view as *panentheist*: they affirm that, though God is 'more than' the world, in some sense the

---

[61] See Spinoza's *Ethics*, especially part I.
[62] See, e.g., Steven Nadler (2023, section 2.1) for some discussion, including whether Spinoza is best read as identifying God as *natura naturans* (nature naturing) or, as Nadler thinks is more likely, both *natura naturans* and *natura naturata* (nature natured). *Natura naturans* and *natura naturata* are not separate orders of being – with one somehow out of nature and one in nature – but dimensions of, or in, the one natural world. Or perhaps they're two ways of looking at the one natural world. For an interesting recent discussion of Spinoza's relevance to contemporary understandings of God and nature, see Moira Gatens (2020).
[63] For a recent discussion of pantheism, see Andrei Buckareff (2022).
[64] Note, however, that Corrington (1998: 171) thinks that 'ecstatic naturalism' affirms 'some finite and fragmentary prospects of transcendence within the dimension of nature natured'.
[65] There is a wide variety of process views, deriving initially from Whitehead and subsequent developments by Charles Hartshorne. For useful introductions, see John Cobb and David Ray Griffin (1976) and Robert Mesle (1993). For a recent survey, focusing on Whitehead and Hartshorne, see David Viney (2022).

world is 'in' God and God is 'in' the world.⁶⁶ Religious naturalism is thus supported at least to the extent that Nature is caught up in the sacredness of the divine, and even, on some views, constitutes 'God's body'.⁶⁷ However, panentheist accounts qualify as one-world-naturalist only if they don't understand God as a supra-natural being. Many process and panentheist views fail this condition.⁶⁸ Arthur Peacocke aims for a viable Christian panentheist naturalism by ruling out any divine supernatural intervention in the natural order. Since Peacocke retains God as a personal being, however, a distinct supra-natural ontological order is still implicated.⁶⁹ Christopher Knight (2005 and 2007) suggests adopting the notion of *inherent* teleology found in Maximus the Confessor's (neo-)Byzantine understanding of God's action and presence in the world. This account is one-world-ist, since it avoids the idea of an external agent or force leading created things to their ends: rather, the divine *Logos*, present in every created thing, is the source of the world's inherent teleological dynamism.

'Ground-of-being' theologies – inspired by Paul Tillich, and holding that God is not 'a' being but 'the ground of being' – have, like most process and panentheist views, also been generally excluded from the family of naturalisms.⁷⁰ But if God is not strictly a being or an entity in Tillich's ontology,

---

⁶⁶ According to F. L. Cross and E. Livingstone (2005: 1221), the standard definition of 'panentheism' is 'the belief that the Being of God includes and penetrates the whole universe, so that every part of it exists in Him, but (as against pantheism) that His Being is more than, and is not exhausted by, the universe'. What's meant by the 'en' ('in') in 'panentheism' (all-in-God-ism') is controversial. Ryan Mullins (2016) initiated a flurry of papers about this. Subsequent attempts to find literal meanings of 'en/in' include Karl Pfeifer (2020) and Joanna Leidenhag (2020). Not all varieties of panentheism are restricted to the Christian tradition. For a wide-ranging historical discussion of the development of panentheism from Plotinus to the present, see John Cooper (2006). For more recent work on Indian panentheist traditions and their connections with Western panentheist conceptions, see Benedict Göcke and Swami Medhananda (2024).

⁶⁷ Panentheists think they offer a better model of the God–world relation, and so of divine transcendence and immanance, than that given by others. They emphasize the intimate relationship between God and the world, often speaking of the world as God's body. See, e.g., Sallie McFague (1990). Different things have been meant by this. Some panentheists accept this model/metaphor, e.g., McFague and Clayton (1997). Note that the idea that the world is God's body isn't restricted to self-identifying panentheists. In a paper presented at the Pantheism and Panentheism Project workshop in Birmingham, UK, on 29 May 2019, Tim Mawson claims that (understood literally) it is a *theist* view.

⁶⁸ Two examples: Hartshorne's (1984) understanding of God as a being unsurpassable except by himself preserves God's supra-natural status even though God's omnipotence is denied. And Philip Clayton's (2008) 'open (kenotic) panentheism' retains a personal God who creates *ex nihilo*, and thus counts as supra-natural.

⁶⁹ See Peacocke (2007b), which is followed in Peacocke (2007a) by ten 'Responses' and Peacocke's 'Reflections' on them. For this kind of criticism of Peacocke's claim to be naturalist, see Clayton (2007: xii).

⁷⁰ Wesley Wildman (2006: 613) distinguishes 'ground of being' theisms from 'determinate entity' theisms, and observes that the former have 'impressive intellectual lineages in all large religious and philosophical traditions'. In rejecting any claim that Tillich's theology is naturalist, Stone

his ground-of-being theology may cohere with an expansive, but still one-world-ist, naturalism. Ground-of-being theologies do run afoul of certain definitions of 'naturalism' – in particular, the Stone-Hardwick-Edwards definition (cited earlier, Section 4.2, note 30) which commits naturalism to holding that the natural world's existence as a whole necessarily has no need of explanation beyond itself. But this definition expresses an overly restrictive notion of 'naturalism', too much in thrall to metaphysical scientific naturalism. The possibility of an expansive one-world-ist naturalism is overlooked, and a religious naturalism is assumed to be essentially 'naturist' in identifying Nature or something within it as religiously ultimate.[71] We should admit as expansive religious naturalisms, then, 'non-naturist' views which posit a transcendent religious ultimate but without implying the existence of any transcendent *being* beyond the natural world – for example, Niels Gregersen's (2014) 'infinity-based' view, according to which God, though not existing as a separate entity, is the ultimate reality rather than Nature. Our own euteleological understanding of theism (on which more later in this section) is also a case in point.

Anyway, as already noted, some contemporary religious naturalists do deploy the concept of God. Henry Nelson Wieman was an early twentieth century example. For Wieman (1946), value is a real force in the world, not reducible to human projections. Wieman rejected the notion of a personal God, but did not dispense with God-talk, using 'God' as a symbol for the 'serendipitous creativity' within the natural world. Wieman says (1946: 17), 'there is a creative process working in our midst which transforms the human mind and the world relative to the human mind ... transformation by this process is always in the direction of the greater good.' Wieman influenced Gordon Kaufman and Karl Peters, both of whom also speak of God as the creativity of the world (see, for example, Kaufman 2001 and Peters 2002). Peters (2022: 23) says:

> God is not something other than the universe. Neither is God throughout the universe but more than the universe. Rather God is one way of understanding the universe. *God is understanding the universe as its creativity.* ... in a dynamical-relational understanding of things, it may be possible to think of *God* and *World* as *two ways of looking at the same thing.*

(2008: 10) says that Tillich's ground of being 'is so ontologically distinct from any being that it is not either the entire world or a process or entity within it. [He then quotes Tillich (1957: 7)] "God as the ground of being infinitely transcends that of which he is the ground".'

[71] See Section 3.1, where we drew the distinction between 'naturist' and 'one-world-ist' religious naturalisms. Naturist views are always one-world-ist, but not conversely: there can be one-world-ist religious naturalisms whose ultimate religious focus transcends anything natural, including Nature as a whole.

It isn't entirely clear how 'realist' is the understanding these religious naturalists have of their God-talk. Talk of 'God' as a symbol might suggest underlying anti-realism, but it could also indicate being broadly in the apophatic tradition whereby God is definitely real, but God's essence is incomprehensible to us. More recently, Ellis's expansive naturalism allows, utilizing Christian resources, for a clearly realist theist religious naturalism. While Ellis doesn't directly address the notion of an overall purpose for reality, her approach is consistent with it.[72]

In discussing what the 'en' in 'panentheism' might mean, Gasser (2019) argues that it is best understood in an agential sense. God is in the world by creating and sustaining it; the world is in God by being the sphere of divine activity. The upshot of Gasser's analysis is (as he points out) that the sharp distinction usually drawn between classical theism and panentheism collapses. One consequence seems to be that if there are varieties of panentheism that can provide a viable religious naturalism, so too might classical theism. And this should not be surprising, too, if Knight is on the right track in arguing that the early Church Fathers and Eastern orthodox traditions have the resources available for a viable form of (theist) naturalism.

It emerges, then, that the classical theist understanding of the Abrahamic traditions may *itself* aptly be regarded as a religious naturalism. That may seem strange, especially to analytic philosophers, who typically assume that theism is virtually definable as holding that God is literally a personal being, who must then be ontologically distinct from the natural world.[73] For classical theists, God is, as Anselm says, that than which a greater cannot be thought (where the relevant kind of greatness is greatness in being and in worth, taken indissolubly together). God cannot therefore be 'a' being belonging to any category or kind of thing, for God is that which *gives being* to all the kinds of things that there are. God may be addressed in personal terms – indeed, Anselm's *Proslogion* is an address to God – and sacred writings, creeds, and teachings use personal language about God to make truth-claims. But God should not be *understood literally* as a personal being, nor as any kind of being at all. Our understanding can only gesture at what God is – for example, by saying with Aquinas, that God

---

[72] See the previously cited works by Ellis at the end of Section 3.3. For an examination of the development of Ellis's conception of God, see Jessica Eastwood (2024a). Eastwood herself defends a 'thinner' version of Ellis's realist religious naturalism. For more on 'thick/thicker' and 'thin/thinner' levels of robustness in naturalistic accounts, see Eastwood (2024b). (Our thanks to an anonymous reviewer for drawing this work to our attention.)

[73] For an exposition of the contrast between this kind of 'theistic personalism' (as he terms it) and classical theism, see Brian Davies (2004). Our brief account of classical theism in the remainder of this paragraph mentions two thinkers from the Christian tradition only, but classical theists are found in all three Abrahamic traditions – for example, Maimonides in Judaism, and Ibn Sina (Avicenna) in Islam.

is 'Being itself' (*ipsum esse subsistens*), though this doesn't capture the 'essence' of God, which is beyond our comprehension. For classical theism, then, in an important sense, God is 'no-thing'.[74] God absolutely transcends all God's creatures, yet God does not relate to them as something – some *thing* – other than them. Rather, God is 'immanently' present with[in] every creature whose existence God sustains, and thus within the entire natural world, forging an indissoluble tie between love of God and love for the natural world. Since God's immanence in creation fits with a transcendence over it that doesn't amount to the transcendence *of a supra-natural being*, the classical theist picture of reality is one-world naturalist.

Classical theism thus has excellent credentials as an expansive religious naturalism that grounds ethical concern for other species and ecosystems. This conclusion is sustained by the evidence of Hebrew scriptural teachings about the need for humanity to care for and restore the creation, and by creation-centred spirituality, especially in the tradition of Saint Francis of Assisi, in Christianity.[75] We'll conclude this subsection, then, by illustrating how a euteleological religious naturalist within the Judaeo-Christian tradition may understand the nature of reality's telic end and supreme good. That such a good would be an integrative good fits with theist emphasis on the *order* of the creation. It also fits with the Christian notion of love (*agapē*) as the highest value: indeed, *agapē* is a leading Christian candidate for the status of the supreme good, for the sake of which everything real exists.

---

[74] How can sentences referring to 'God' possibly be true, if God is not literally a being of any kind? The answer is straightforward: God *is* a thing in the broadest sense, but *not* in the mundane sense of a being or an entity. Grasping this answer – and its straightforwardness – isn't so easy! To elaborate briefly: God is a thing that must be referred to in describing ultimate reality according to the theist worldview (as being 'the God-way'). But God's thing-ness is no more than the barest reference-securing kind of thing-ness: God is *not* a mundane thing of the type that has properties, stands in relation with other things and instantiates general kinds. 'Bare' referent-status thing-ness can be understood only as *an analogizing construction* from mundane thingness. God's bare thingness thus involves a cognitive construction, but *not* a *fictionalising* construction, since God's bare thingness is the flip-side of God's *reality* being so great that nothing greater could even be conceived. For more discussion, see Bishop and Perszyk (2023, ch. 4), where we deploy this kind of account in defending euteleological metaphysics as apt for the theist worldview. See also *International Journal for Philosophy of Religion* 96(3), 2024, 223–54, where the alleged 'obscurity and shock' of a 'no-thing' God is a central topic in a book symposium on our *God, Purpose, and Reality*.

[75] For a wide-ranging study of Hebrew Bible texts supporting humanity's kinship with the wider creation, in which humans are understood as only one kind of person amongst others, see, e.g., Mari Joerstad's (2019). Saint Francis was declared the patron saint of ecology by Pope John Paul II in 1979. And in 2015 *Laudato Si'*, the second encyclical of Pope Francis, was published with the sub-title 'On care for our common home'. For a wide-ranging, contextual study and critical assessment of Saint Francis's views on nature, see, e.g., Roger Sorrell (2009). For some examples of discussions of ecotheology from an Islamic perspective see Soumaya Pernilla Ouis (1998), and Moustapha Gueye and Najma Mohamed (2023).

For *agapē* to fit this role, the Christian naturalist will need to champion the idea that *agapē* is an integrative good which consists in *right relationship*, harmonious and just (or well-ordered) – a notion that extends beyond God-to-human and human-to-human relationships to all creatures quite generally. Discussions of *agapē* for almost a century now have been heavily influenced by Anders Nygren (1932 and 1938/9). Nygren drew a very sharp distinction between *agapē* and *eros* (with apparently no discussion of *philia*, usually translated 'friendship'), and also saw *agapē* as essentially self-sacrificial. In our view, *agapē requires* proper self-regard (recall the phrase that modifies the second 'great commandment', 'Love your neighbour as yourself'). *Agapē* is also compatible with erotic relationships of the properly mutual kind. Sometimes, self-sacrifice may be required for right relationship, but it's mistaken to see *agapē* as *necessarily* careless of self-regard. Martin D'Arcy (1947: 245), for example, thought that in *agapē* there is a 'perfect correspondence between taking and giving, self-regard and self-surrender', and he grounds *agapē* in the mutual love of the Trinity. Feminist ethicists have gone further in stressing a need for proper self-regard and have explored mutuality as the most appropriate image of Christian love.[76] According to Susan Bratton (1992: 4), 'Christianity clearly holds love to be the source of right relationship toward both God and one's neighbor; yet it remains unclear how Christian love should be extended toward the environment.' Classic works on Christian love such as Nygren's don't address this issue.

Bratton discusses some contemporary attempts by theologians to deal with the implications of Christian love for environmental ethics, as well as some key Biblical texts that give strong support to the idea that (divine) *agapē* (as well as the covenant-love of the Old Testament) extends toward or applies to nature, not just to humanity. She then argues that *agapē* can apply to human love of nature, and is indeed preferable to *eros*. (There is a danger that *eros* towards nature, understood as wanting to possess and use it, with no mutuality, and so no *agapē*, leads to the exploitation and denigration of nature – though perhaps *agapē* is consistent with an 'aesthetic' *eros* directed at the beauty of the natural world.) In Bratton's view, *agapē* is the right attitude for a Christian to have towards nature. What we are suggesting is that a Christian religious naturalist may understand *agapē* as the supreme good, given the broadest possible account of *agapē* as right relationship. One advantage of such an account is that the essence of the supreme good remains – as we noted earlier seems fitting – incomprehensible, in the sense that humans cannot gain theoretical mastery of it. Instead, the emphasis is thrown onto *practical acquaintance* with instantiations of *agapē* in

---

[76] See, e.g., Barbara Hilkbert Andolsen (1981).

human experience. And, when *agapē* is given its broadest scope in a Christian naturalism, there will be the recognition that *agapē* can be instantatiated (or not) in human relations with other species and with ecosystems. The tradition (as it develops) may enlarge its stock of narratives with exemplars of agapeistic relationships (or their lack) between humans and their wider natural environment. For the Christian naturalist, humans have the potential to instantiate and participate in the supreme good, but the supreme good should not be seen as open solely to human fulfilment.[77]

6 Conclusion: Challenges for Religious Naturalists

Religious naturalism faces challenges. At its conceptual heart, there's the challenge of accommodating a satisfyingly religious outlook with a meaningfully naturalist commitment. Both religion and naturalism take an overall view of reality – a perspective on how things are as a whole. There are differing conceptions of naturalism, but some desiderata seem basic. A naturalist orientation holds that the natural world is the only – concrete – world there is, and that we must take seriously what empirical scientific methods (albeit fallibly) confirm about what that one natural world is like. An austere naturalism goes beyond these basics by holding that there can be nothing more to the natural world than could in principle be disclosed by science. Many adherents to that kind of metaphysical scientific naturalism take their naturalism to be the antithesis of a religious outlook (they are 'naturalist-atheists', or perhaps better to say, '*a-religious* naturalists'). Other equally passionate naturalists, however, are *religious* naturalists, holding that their naturalism can accommodate a religious overall view of reality.

Religious naturalists are typically nature-focused, and regard natural human feelings of awe and gratitude towards nature as more than the merely emotional phenomena which a-religious-naturalists hold them to be. Religious naturalists take such feelings to carry significance *for the way the world is*. But they locate what they take these religious feelings to signify *within* the one natural world: they do not posit any supra-natural being as the object of ultimate awe and gratitude. We have called this stance 'one-worldism': for all the diversity of existents, ultimately all that concretely exists

---

[77] This point may apply to non-Western religious traditions as well. For example, the Christian notion of *agapē* appears close to the Confucian notion of *jen*, and, according to Xinzhong Yao (1996: 23), 'Confucian love is universally applicable and extends the idea of brotherhood to all creatures in the cosmos.' Another analogue of *agapē* might be the notion of *karuṇā* (often translated as compassion), which is found in Indian traditions (Hinduism, Buddhism, Sikhism, and Jainism).

belongs to the same ontological order, to be identified with the natural world accessible to us through experience.

There's a range of perspectives which may reasonably be described as religious naturalisms. We haven't tried to establish that any of them are true. We've assumed that any religious naturalist worldview, like any total perspective on reality, would have to be accepted by faith going beyond, though not against, what is shown likely to be true by publicly checkable empirical evidence. Our focus has rather been on understanding *the content* of religious naturalisms, and the ways they combine different conceptions of both 'religiousness' and 'naturalism'.[78] We've suggested that it is useful to distinguish types of religious naturalism according to how metaphysically ambitious they are. Naturalism curbs metaphysical ambition. Austere metaphysical scientific naturalism leaves no room for anything concretely real that couldn't be disclosed by empirical scientific methods. That kind of naturalism *may* be religious, though only in a relatively 'thin' or metaphysically constrained way. Metaphysical scientific naturalists may accept that feelings of wonder aroused by nature signify *something* about reality – but no more than the fact that features of the natural world have the 'response-dependent' disposition to produce (under certain conditions) 'apt' feelings of awe and gratitude in animals of the sort that humans are. For some naturalists, that may be enough to satisfy their religiousness, especially if there is something religious about an austere naturalist stance itself (as the religious-like zeal with which it is often held may suggest).

But it's a moveable feast whether or not a specific outlook counts as a satisfyingly religious one. One person's religious promptings may be met by an overall stance on reality that wouldn't suit another's religious aspirations. Religious naturalists – indeed, naturalists generally – typically affirm a set of values that include human respect and sustainable care for other species and ecosystems. More robust forms of religious naturalism make metaphysical posits that secure the 'objective' reality of such values and provide an account of ultimate reality that makes it reasonable to live by those values hopefully,

---

[78] 'Demarcation' debates about what counts as 'strict' or 'proper' religious naturalism (or about who's really in the religious naturalist camp and who's not) thus strike us as somewhat pointless. Those who, for what they take to be good reasons, favour *particular* understandings of what's required for being religious or for being committed to naturalism, will naturally demarcate 'proper' religious naturalism *relative to* those understandings. But we think that claims to settle this demarcation issue can do so only relatively to assumptions which others may – quite reasonably – fail to share. This is not to deny, of course, the importance of considering what type of religious naturalism (if any) may merit our commitment as an overall practical orientation to reality. Debates about what kind of religious naturalism may be adequate in that respect are certainly worth having! For more discussion relevant to matters of demarcation see, e.g., Stone (2008, ch. 1, and 2018), Mikael Stenmark (2013) and Drees (2018).

despite obstacles and costs. Many religious naturalists think that taking our responses to nature seriously requires accepting something *intrinsically* sacred about nature (or about key features of it). To satisfy this requirement, these religious naturalists will need to affirm value realism. That may push beyond anything metaphysical scientific naturalists can accept (the question is controversial). But those boundaries are definitely breached if a religious naturalism posits, not only value realism, but a vision of ultimate reality that explains why the objective values are as they are, and also explains why we may reasonably hope (ultimately) to do well through living by those values. Such a robust religiousness could attach to a naturalist worldview only if it may remain meaningfully naturalist while expanding beyond a purely science-generated view of the world.

An *expansive* one-world-ist naturalism is indeed possible – or so we have maintained. Naturalism has to be one-world-ist, but it need not hold that the one natural world necessarily coincides with the world as empirical science could describe it. An expansive naturalism can thus be more robustly religious provided that the metaphysical posits it makes beyond what science could disclose are at least consistent with what science *does* disclose (something that can, of course, be judged, and judged fallibly, only with respect to our current best empirical theories).

A one-world-ist stance faces this question: what is it that makes the natural world *one*? Metaphysical scientific naturalists will say that the natural world's 'principle of unity' is accessibility to being known through empirical scientific methods. Or, seeking something seemingly more ontological, they will say that everything natural 'falls under the laws of nature' (as disclosed by scientific methods, of course). The religiously inclined find this proposal inadequate to their sense of human existence as part of something very much greater (for them, man is decidedly not 'the measure of all things'). They typically also think that constraining the one world to what's governed by laws of nature would leave no room for the purposiveness of human existence, nor for the values implied by the ethical intuitions that human lives *matter* and that it *matters* how human lives are lived (in the recognition, in particular, that it is not *only* human lives that matter). An expansive religious naturalism of the more robust kind thus needs a principle of suitably wider scope to secure the oneness of the natural world.

We have proposed that expansive religious naturalists may hold that the oneness of the natural world consists in its having *inherently* an overall purpose for which it exists. Various attempts have been made at naturalist accounts of cosmic purpose. Our specific proposal is that this should be done by taking its purposiveness to be a *transcendent* feature of the natural world. This transcendent feature is not scientifically discoverable but is rather a metaphysical posit, consistent with what we know empirically, but driven by practical and ethical considerations that recommend a way of living oriented by a faith that takes the natural world to be purposive. We have suggested a *euteleological* approach to understanding the transcendent purposiveness of the natural world without positing any concrete transcendent beings (such as a divine personal creator). According to euteleology, to be real is to be inherently directed upon realizing an ultimate end (*telos*) which is the good for reality as such, and, therefore, the *supreme* good; and the Universe itself (i.e., all contingent existents) exists ultimately because it realizes that supreme good within it, in multiple, perhaps infinitely multiple, ways. In making this suggestion, we are doing no more than indicating a potentially promising way to specify an expansive, one-world-ist, religious naturalism. We haven't tried to prove that the notion of a cosmic purpose has to be deployed, nor that, if it is, it must be understood in the euteleological way. However, we have aimed to show that, if a euteleological worldview is viable, then the challenge of articulating a robustly religious outlook that satisfies the constraints of one-world-ist naturalism may be met.

But could a euteleological one-world-ist naturalism really be viable? Could it be truly *religiously* effective? Any practically effective religious naturalism must provide resources for living out its religious commitment. These resources include individual and communal ways of developing and expressing that commitment, exemplars and exponents of 'the faith', and institutions for facilitating what's needed. The practice of religious commitment thus requires some form of religious community. Should religious naturalists find their community within existing traditions? Or do they need to found new religious communities, which may draw on existing traditions yet without adhering to any?

The answer may depend on the type of religious naturalism. Perhaps the more austere religious naturalists may find all the 'religious' community they need in the practice of science itself. More robust religious naturalists will have a greater need for specifically religious community, practices, and doctrine. We have mentioned earlier some examples of what is available outside traditional religious contexts to meet this need (see Section 2.4, notes 9 and 10). But religious effectiveness may require drawing on the resources of existing religious traditions. In particular, those who take a euteleological approach need to have an adequate idea of what that overall purpose and supreme good is – sufficient, at least, to develop a practical understanding of what it is to live hopefully and well in a world whose purpose is to realize that good. Such an understanding may be found in established religious traditions, including the

Abrahamic ones. Traditional resources, according to some at least, may no longer be fit for purpose, but starting completely afresh is a tall order.

A religiously effective euteleological religious naturalism may draw, then, on traditional resources – in particular, in specifying the posited overall purpose and supreme good. We have argued that such a good would have to be an *integrative* good, bringing a wide diversity of goods (goods for different kinds of things) into a harmony of right relationship with each other. The idea of such an integrative good, we have suggested, may be implicit in some non-theist religious traditions and in Indigenous worldviews, and is definitely found in the creation-focused spirituality of the Abrahamic traditions. In particular, we've suggested that the Christian notion of *agapē* – love of the kind that, on its broadest understanding, consists in right relationship – may serve to specify for the euteleological religious naturalist the supreme good and ultimate end of all things.

So much for a brief concluding summary of how we think we have, in the preceding sections, met the basic challenge of showing that a robustly religious naturalism is possible by proposing a euteleological account of one natural world existing to fufil, and because it does fulfil, its overall purpose. To wind things up, we'll mention two significant reasons why it may be thought that this euteleological proposal doesn't do the job. The first challenge is that a perspective cannot be authentically religious unless it offers a way of overcoming the fear of death – and that, it may be thought, requires some form of immortality. Making room for immortality, however, seems inadmissible, not merely by scientific naturalism, but also by any one-world-ist naturalism, however 'expansive'. As John Hick observes, a naturalism that says there is no concrete world but the natural world seems to be very bad news for people in history who, through no fault of their own, fall short of realizing their human potential.[79]

One-world-ist naturalists seeking a religious perspective that offers better news and quietens the fear of death might perhaps draw on traditions which posit reincarnation, which seems feasible within the one world, at least on a suitably expansive view of it. However, *complete* compensation and fulfilment

---

[79] Hick (2004: 23–4) writes:

> They [naturalists, whether secular or religious] ought frankly to acknowledge that if they are right the human situation is irredeemably bleak and painful for vast numbers of people. For – if they are right – in the case of that innumerable multitude whose quality of life has been rendered predominantly negative by pain, anxiety, extreme deprivation, oppression, or whose lives have been cut off in childhood or youth, there is no chance of their ever participating in an eventual fulfilment of their human potential. There is no possibility of this vast century-upon-century tragedy being part of a much larger process which leads ultimately to limitless good.

would require eventual release from the cycle of death and rebirth, as typically posited in traditions that believe in reincarnation. But that kind of ultimate fulfilment apparently implies a 'destination' for souls beyond the one natural world.[80]

Religious naturalists who take the euteleological approach face the same difficulty. Two possible strategies seem available to counter the charge that, in ruling out immortality in some permanent future realm beyond the natural world, any naturalist perspective will inevitably fail to count as 'sufficiently religious'. The first strategy is to make a *religious* case for embracing mortality: euteleologists may say that our lives having an end, just as their having a beginning, is in accordance with how things ought to be in the eutelic Universe in which the supreme good is realized. That first response, by itself, may be unsatisfyingly austere – what of those who die in childhood, for example? Is their being so cut off really 'in accordance with how things ought to be'?

The second strategy is to accept that adequately religious views about ultimate fulfilment must indeed involve transcending mortality, but then go on to argue that mortality can be transcended *within* the one natural world. Whether this view can be sustained is moot. To remain one-world-ist, the idea of transcending mortality needs to avoid commitment to any literal eschatological consummation which would have to be 'other-worldly'. Perhaps the euteleologist can say that the mortal takes on immortality whenever, within the historical natural world, mortals participate in realizing the supreme good? Maybe the two strategies can be combined by holding that mortality can be transcended only when its reality is wholly accepted? To give these ideas real charge, it may be necessary to draw on the Abrahamic religious traditions from which they are in fact derived. The promise of eternal life in these traditions is for a radically transformed self that overcomes self-centredness, and recognizes that 'we are dust, and unto dust we shall return' (see Genesis 3:19). With self-centredness overcome, so too is the desire for the endless persistence of the individual self.[81]

---

[80] Corrington has argued, however, that a 'capacious religious naturalism' can accommodate within one world an understanding of the human soul as eternal 'at both ends' (see Corrington 2007: 506–7). This would seem to be a possibility only if the contingently existing Universe is itself eternal, which it would presumably be if the Universe is an infinite 'multiverse' of 'big bang' initiated spatio-temporal universes like ours. Steinhart's Platonist paganism also accommodates unlimited reincarnations: see his (2025b) and our reply, Bishop and Perszyk (2025b).

[81] Hardwick (1996: 286) writes:

> At the prophetic center of Christianity is the critique of egoism and salvation is conceived as its overcoming. It is utterly implausible, therefore, that at its center it also promises a subjective survival of self that offers solace and encouragement to some of our most egoistic impulses. Thus, if I am correct, the "death" that is overcome

True joys are found by fixing our hearts on what really matters – namely, the fulfilment of the divine purposes in creation (that is, for euteleologists, realizations of the supreme good).

We've disclaimed any attempt to show that euteleological religious naturalism is actually true, but it will have to be *possibly true* for it to be reasonably accepted. A further challenge to this kind of religious naturalism, then, is that it is *not possible* that reality should be inherently directed upon the supreme good, given the facts about the existence of evil. This 'problem of evil' challenge besets any religious worldview that posits a vision of ultimate reality favourable to pursuit of the good and claiming resources for overcoming evil. In a nutshell, whatever it is about reality that is supposed to give ultimate sovereignty to the good looks unlikely to be true if not outrightly impossible given the existence of evil – or, anyway, given the existence of the types, amounts, and distributions of evils that do in fact exist.

Euteleological religious naturalism has a response to this challenge which we think is effective. First, a claim is made about what evil is – namely, that evil is *privation* of the good, in the sense of a lack of the good that there ought to be. Evidently, on this understanding, the existence of evil is not logically inconsistent with (in fact it presupposes) reality's being directed upon the good.[82] A second claim needs to be made, however – since the challenger may ask how evils are possible in a world directed towards realizing the good even if they are understood as privations of the good there ought to be. In response, the euteleologist's second claim is simply to say that, for all we know, there are inherent limitations in the 'business' of making the supreme good concretely, finitely, and contingently real. Furthermore, those limitations, as a matter of statistical if not logical necessity, result in things sometimes not possessing properties which they ought to have if they are to contribute to realizing, or to participate in realizing, the supreme good. The ideal good becoming finitely real, in other words, has the existence of evils as a side effect. These responses might leave still unanswered the objection that evil is logically inconsistent with reality's directedness upon the good if that were supposedly guaranteed by

---

[according to Christian teaching] is not physical death ... [but rather] spiritual death which resides in inauthentic existence and is the opposite of the life we have in faith.

[82] This account of evil is borrowed directly from the classical theist teaching that evil is *privatio boni*. This doctrine is widely dismissed by contemporary analytic philosophers as implying the absurd view that evil is a 'mere absence'. In fact, on this account, evils are always presences – namely, real features of the things that are or suffer evil – but they are 'presences' that, not merely lack something good, but lack the good *that those things ought to have* on a teleological understanding of their reality. For a general discussion of evil and suffering that places the 'privationist' account of evil in a wider context see Bishop (2021).

a supreme agent with ultimate control over existence. But, of course, a euteleological naturalism rejects that scenario.

It may still be urged that the facts about evils in the world (understood more neutrally as simply bad, or very bad, things) make it reasonable not to accept the euteleological claim that reality is inherently 'for' the good. If euteleology were treated as a hypothesis to be settled by a dispassionate consideration of the evidence, the rational upshot may indeed be to suspend judgment on its truth. But euteleology is not a quasi-scientific explanatory hypothesis: it is an option for an overall stance on ultimate reality that secures values by which we are to live in the hope of fulfilment (something beyond anything science could disclose). Reflection on evil may, of course, leave us unmotivated to make a faith-venture in favour of such a view: but, if the response described in the previous paragraph is adequate, the facts about evil cannot exclude a euteleological religious naturalist option for those who are – as William James would say, 'passionally'– motivated to adopt it.[83]

Questions about evil, death, and immortality are at the heart of worldviews which purport to serve the functions we have called 'robustly' religious. We have indicated how these questions might be dealt with by the particular, euteleological, form of 'cosmic purpose' naturalism on which we have focused. More needs to be said.[84] For present purposes, it is enough to have shown that robust religious functions – such as securing hopeful pursuit of the good in the face of evil, and overcoming the fear of death – may not necessarily require the resources of a supra-naturalist worldview that appeals to an ontological order of perfected concrete existence beyond the natural order. Naturalism may be religious in a solid enough sense: expanding the reality of the natural world to include metaphysical elements of transcendence sufficient to support 'thicker' religious functions may be achievable without breaking the key naturalist desideratum of one integrated world, the natural world.

However, the kind of guarantees many people seek from religion may not be secured under this 'one-world-ist' constraint. Religious naturalists must accept that their religiousness, at its most robust, cannot offer guarantees that require perfect goodness to have ultimate agential control over reality. But religious

---

[83] Faith is possible only for those motivated to make the necessary venture to commit to the truth of an overall orientation to reality beyond the reach of any purely rational assessment of publicly available evidence. That motivation – evidently! – cannot arise from the rational force of a body of public evidence. Such a motivation James describes as belonging to our 'passional' or 'non-intellectual' nature (1956 [1897]: 11). But, as noted earlier (Section 2.4), James effectively made it a criterion of reasonable faith that what is prompted by our non-intellectual nature should cohere with the reasonable judgments our rational intellect makes about the world.

[84] For more discussion of ideas about eternal life from a euteleological perspective, see Bishop and Perszyk (2022). For elaboration and further defence of the euteleologist's response to the problem of evil, see Bishop and Perszyk (2023, ch. 5).

naturalists may pose the question whether it is religiously admirable to seek such guarantees, especially given that a worldview that provides them must locate ultimate worth and ultimate human destiny somewhere other than the natural world. Do we not do better, religiously, if we take the natural world disclosed to our experience, with its unimaginable vastness and diversity, to be the one location for all that concretely exists and really matters? Isn't such a one-world stance something that's needed in overcoming human individual egoism and human 'speciesism' and in placing us into right relationship with our wider environment? And won't a *religious* naturalism give us the right appreciation both of the value, and of the limits, of our sensory-experience-based scientific understanding of the world?

References

Allen, C., Bekoff, M., and Lauder, G. V., eds. (1998). *Nature's Purposes: Analyses of Function and Design in Biology*. Cambridge, MA: MIT Press.

Allen, C. and Neal, J. (2020). Teleological notions in biology. In E. N. Zalta, ed., *The Stanford Encyclopedia of Philosophy* (Spring 2020 Edition). https://plato.stanford.edu/archives/spr2020/entries/teleology-biology/.

Andolsen, B. H. (1981). Agape in feminist ethics. *Journal of Religious Ethics* **9**(1), 69–83. www.jstor.org/stable/40014924.

Ayer, A. J. (1952 [1936]). *Language, Truth, and Logic*. Mineola, NY: Dover Publications.

Beckett, J. (2017). *The Path of Paganism: An Experience-Based Guide to Modern Pagan Practice*. Woodbury, MN: Llewellyn Publications.

Bishop, J. (2007). *Believing by Faith: An Essay in the Epistemology and Ethics of Religious Belief*. Oxford: Clarendon Press.

Bishop, J. (2010). Secular spirituality and the logic of giving thanks. *Sophia* **49**(4), 523–34. http://doi:10.1007/s11841-010-0216-2.

Bishop, J. (2021). Evil and suffering. In S. Goetz and C. Taliaferro, eds., *The Encyclopedia of Philosophy of Religion*. Hoboken, NJ: John Wiley and Sons, Inc. http://doi:10.1002/9781119009924.eopr0136.

Bishop, J. (2023). Reasonable faith and reasonable fideism. *Religious Studies* **59**(3), 394–409. http://doi:10.1017/S0034412522000282.

Bishop, J. and Perszyk, K. (2017). The divine atttributes and non-personal conceptions of God. *Topoi* **36**(4), 609–21. http://doi:10.1007/s11245-016-9394-z.

Bishop, J. and Perszyk, K. (2022). A-personal conceptions of God and the Christian promise of eternal life. In G. Gasser and S. Kittle, eds., *The Divine Nature: Personal and A-Personal Perspectives*. New York: Routledge, pp. 251–68.

Bishop, J. and Perszyk, K. (2023). *God, Purpose, and Reality: A Euteleological Understanding of Theism*. Oxford: Oxford University Press.

Bishop, J. and Perszyk, K. (2025a). Varieties of religious naturalism: A conceptual investigation. *Neue Zeitschrift für Systematische Theologie und Religionsphilosophie* **67**(2), 129–49. http://doi:10.1515/nzsth-2024-0063.

Bishop, J. and Perszyk, K. (2025b). Replies to Gasser, Schellenberg, and Steinhart. *Neue Zeitschrift für Systematische Theologie und Religionsphilosophie* **67**(2), 169–80. http://doi:10.1515/nzsth-2025-0030.

References

Bishop, J. and Perszyk, K. (forthcoming), Ultimism and euteleology. In K. Viertbauer, ed., *Rethinking Religion with J. L. Schellenberg*. London: Bloomsbury.

Bratton, S. P. (1992). Loving nature: Eros or agape? *Environmental Ethics* **14**(1), 3–25. https://doi.org/10.5840/enviroethics199214137.

Brennan, A. and Lo, N. Y. S. (2024). Environmental ethics. In E. N. Zalta and U. Nodelman, eds., *The Stanford Encyclopedia of Philosophy* (Summer 2024 Edition). https://plato.stanford.edu/archives/sum2024/entries/ethics-environmental.

Brock, R. and Kampourakis, K. (2023). A justification of legitimate teleological explanations in physics education. *Science & Education* **32**(4), 927–45. http://doi:10.1007/s11191-022-00358-8.

Broome, J. (2012). *Climate Matters: Ethics in a Warming World*. New York: W. W. Norton.

Brüntrup, G. and Jaskolla, L., eds. (2017). *Panpsychism: Contemporary Perspectives*. Oxford: Oxford University Press.

Buckareff, A. (2022). *Pantheism*. Cambridge: Cambridge University Press. http://doi:10.1017/9781108558266.

Chakravartty, A. (2017). Scientific realism. In E. N. Zalta, ed., *The Stanford Encyclopedia of Philosophy* (Summer 2017 Edition). https://plato.stanford.edu/archives/sum2017/entries/scientific-realism/.

Clayton, P. (1997). *God and Contemporary Science*. Grand Rapids, MI: Eerdmans Publishing.

Clayton, P. (2007). Editor's introduction. In *All That Is: A Naturalistic Faith for the Twenty-First Century*. Minneapolis, MN: Fortress Press, pp. xi–xvi.

Clayton, P. (2008). Open panentheism and *creatio ex nihilo*. *Process Studies* **37**(1), 166–83. http://doi:10.2307/44797246.

Cobb, J. B. and Griffin, D. R. (1976). *Process Theology: An Introductory Exposition*. Louisville, KY: Westminster John Knox Press.

Colyvan, M., Garfield, J. L., and Priest, G. (2005). Problems with the argument from fine tuning. *Synthese* **145**(3), 325–38. http://doi:10.1007/s11229-005-6195-0.

Cooper, J. W. (2006). *Panentheism: The Other God of the Philosophers: From Plato to the Present*. Grand Rapids, MI: Baker Academic.

Corrington, R. S. (1998). Empirical theology and its divergence from process thought. In R. A. Badham, ed., *Introduction to Christian Theology: Contemporary North American Perspectives*. Louisville, KY: Westminster John Knox Press, pp. 166–79.

Corrington, R. S. (2007). Deep pantheism. *Journal for the Study of Religion, Nature and Culture* **1**(4), 503–7. http://doi:10.1558/jsrnc.v1i4.503.

Cox, J. L. (2014). The debate over Io as the pre-Christian Māori supreme being. In *The Invention of God in Indigenous Societies*. London: Routledge, pp. 35–66.

Crosby, D. A. (2002). *A Religion of Nature*. Albany, NY: State University of New York Press.

Crosby, D. A. (2003). Naturism as a form of religious naturalism. *Zygon* **38**(1), 117–20. http://doi:10.1111/1467-9744.00484.

Crosby, D. A. (2007). Perspectives – on religious naturalism: A case for a religion of nature. *Journal for the Study of Religion, Nature and Culture* **1**(4), 489–502. http://doi:10.1558/jsrnc.v1i4.489.

Crosby, D. A. (2013). Religious naturalism. In C. Meister and P. Copan, eds., *The Routledge Companion to Philosophy of Religion*, 2nd edn. New York: Routledge, pp. 744–53.

Crosby, D. A. (2015). *Nature as Sacred Ground: A Metaphysics for Religious Naturalism*. Albany, NY: State University of New York Press.

Crosby, D. A. (2023). *Evolutionary Emergence of Purposive Goals and Values: A Naturalistic Teleology*. Albany, NY: State University of New York Press.

Crosby, D. A. and Stone, J. A., eds. (2018). *The Routledge Handbook of Religious Naturalism*. New York: Routledge.

Cross, F. L. and Livingstone, E., eds. (2005). *Oxford Dictionary of the Christian Church*. Oxford: Oxford University Press.

D'Arcy, M. C. (1947). *The Mind and Heart of Love Lion and Unicorn: A Study in Eros and Agape*. New York: Henry Holt and Company.

Davies, B. (2004). *An Introduction to the Philosophy of Religion*, 3rd edn. Oxford: Oxford University Press.

Dawkins, R. (2006). *The God Delusion*. London: Bantam Press.

De Caro, M. and Macarthur, D. (2010). Introduction: Science, naturalism, and the problem of normativity. In M. De Caro and D. Macarthur, eds., *Naturalism and Normativity*. New York: Columbia University Press, pp. 1–19.

De Caro, M. and Macarthur, D., eds. (2022). *The Routledge Handbook of Liberal Naturalism*. London: Routledge.

De Cruz, H. (2020). Awe and wonder in scientific practice: Implications for the relationship between science and religion. In M. Fuller et al., eds., *Issues in Science and Theology: Nature – and Beyond*. Cham: Springer, pp. 155–68.

Deloria, Jr., V. (1999). *Spirit and Reason: The Vine Deloria, Jr., Reader*. Edited by S. Scinta, K. Foehner, and B. Deloria. Wheat Ridge, CO: Fulcrum Publishing.

Deloria, Jr., V. (2003). *God is Red: A Native View of Religion, 30th Anniversary Edition*. Wheat Ridge, CO: Fulcrum Publishing.

Dennett, D. C. (2006). *Breaking the Spell: Religion as a Natural Phenomenon*. New York: Viking Penguin.

Drees, W. B. (1996). *Religion, Science and Naturalism*. Cambridge: Cambridge University Press.

Drees, W. B. (2018). Religious naturalism and its near neighbors. In D. A. Crosby and J. A. Stone, eds., *The Routledge Handbook of Religious Naturalism*. London: Routledge, pp. 19–30.

Driver, J. (2022). The history of utilitarianism. In E. N. Zalta and U. Nodelman, eds., *The Stanford Encyclopedia of Philosophy*, Winter 2022 Edition. https://plato.stanford.edu/archives/win2022/entries/utilitarianism-history/.

Dubs, H. H. (1943). Religious naturalism – an evaluation. *Journal of Religion* **23**(4), 258–65. http://doi:10.1086/483044.

Dworkin, R. (2013). *Religion Without God*. Cambridge, MA: Harvard University Press.

Dyke, H. (2023). Taking taniwha seriously: A neutral realist interpretation of Kingsbury's approach. *Asian Journal of Philosophy* **2**(1), 1–9. http://doi:10.1007/s44204-022-00056.

Eastwood J. (2024a). Theistic expansive naturalism: Which God? *Religious Studies* **60**(3), 413–27. http://doi:10.1017/S0034412523000112.

Eastwood J. (2024b). *Transcending Fictionalism: God, Minimalism and Realism*. London: Bloomsbury.

Edwards, R. B. (1972). *Reason and Religion: Introduction to the Philosophy of Religion*. New York: Harcourt.

Eklund, M. (2024). Fictionalism. In E. N. Zalta and U. Nodelman, eds., *The Stanford Encyclopedia of Philosophy* (Spring 2024 Edition). https://plato.stanford.edu/archives/spr2024/entries/fictionalism/.

Ellis, F. (2014). *God, Value, and Nature*. Oxford: Oxford University Press.

Ellis, F. (2019). Between orthodox theism and materialist atheism. In P. Draper, ed., *Current Controversies in Philosophy of Religion*. New York: Routledge, pp. 146–59.

Ellis, F. (2020). True naturalism, goodness, and God. *Think* **19**(56), 109–20. http://doi:10.1017/S1477175620000263.

Ellis, F. (2022). Liberal naturalism and God. In M. De Caro and D. Macarthur, eds., *The Routledge Handbook of Liberal Naturalism*. London: Routledge, pp. 218–26.

Gasser, G. (2019). God's omnipresence in the world: On possible meanings of 'en' in panentheism. *International Journal for Philosophy of Religion* **85**(1), 43–62. http://doi:10.1007/s11153-018-9695-9.

Gasser, G. (2025) Hope abiding: Comment on 'Varieties of religious naturalism: A conceptual investigation'. *Neue Zeitschrift für Systematische Theologie und Religionsphilosophie* **67**(2), 150–57. https://doi.org/10.1515/nzsth-2025-0028.

Gatens, M. (2020). The barking dog and the mind of God. *Australasian Philosophical Review* **4**(3), 216–24. http://doi:10.1080/24740500.2021.1962648.

Göcke, B. P. and Medhananda, S., eds. (2024). *Panentheism in Indian and Western Thought: Cosmopolitan Interventions*. London: Routledge.

Goff, P. (2023). *Why? The Purpose of the Universe*. Oxford: Oxford University Press.

Goodenough, U. (2023). *The Sacred Depths of Nature: How Life has Emerged and Evolved*. New York: Oxford University Press. Second edition [first edition 1998].

Goodenough, U., Cavanaugh, M., and Macalister, T. (2018). Bringing religious naturalists together online. In J. A. Stone and D. A. Crosby, eds., *The Routledge Handbook of Religious Naturalism*. London: Routledge, pp. 310–16.

Gowans, C. W. (2018). The Buddha's message. In E. D. Klemke and S. M. Cahn, eds., *The Meaning of Life: A Reader*, fourth edition. Oxford: Oxford University Press, pp. 27–34.

Gregersen, N. (2014). Naturalism in the mirror of religion. *Philosophy, Theology and the Sciences* **1**(1), 99–129. http://doi:10.1628/219728314X13946985797032.

Gueye, M. K. and Mohamed, N. (2023). An Islamic perspective on ecotheology and sustainability. In L. Hufmagel, ed., *Ecotheology – Sustainability and Religions of the World*. London: IntechOpen.

Hardwick, C. D. (1996). *Events of Grace: Naturalism, Existentialism, and Theology*. Cambridge: Cambridge University Press.

Hardwick, C. D. (2003). Religious naturalism today. *Zygon* **38**(1), 111–16. http://doi:10.1111/1467-9744.00483.

Harmsworth, G. R. and Awatere, S. (2013). Indigenous Māori knowledge and perspectives of ecosystems. In J. R. Dymond, ed., *Ecosystem Services in New Zealand*. Lincoln, NZ: Manaaki Whenua Press, pp. 274–86.

Hartshorne, C. (1984). *Omnipotence and Other Theological Mistakes*. Albany, NY: State University of New York Press.

Harvey, G. (2005). *Animism: Respecting the Living World*. New York: Columbia University Press.

Haught, J. F. (2003). Is nature enough? No. *Zygon* **38**(4), 769–82. http://doi:10.1111/j.1467-9744.2003.00538.x.

Haught, J. F. (2006). *Is Nature Enough? Meaning and Truth in the Age of Science*. Cambridge: Cambridge University Press.

Hegel, G. W. F. (2019 [1807]). *The Phenomenology of Spirit*. Edited and translated by T. Pinkard and M. Baur. Cambridge: Cambridge University Press.

Hick, J. (2004). *The Fifth Dimension: An Exploration of the Spiritual Realm*. London: Oneworld Publications. Second edition [first edition 1999].

Hogue, M. S. (2010). *The Promise of Religious Naturalism*. Lanham, MD: Rowman & Littlefield.

Hogue, M. (2014). Religion without God: The way of religious naturalism. *The Fourth R* **27**(3), 3–6; 15–16.

Hume, D. (1993 [1779]). *Dialogues Concerning Natural Religion*. In J. C. A. Gaskin, ed., *Principal Writings on Religion*. New York: Oxford University Press.

Hursthouse, R. (1999). *On Virtue Ethics*. Oxford: Clarendon Press.

James, W. (1956 [1897]). The will to believe. In *The Will to Believe and Other Essays in Popular Philosophy, and Human Immortality*. New York: Dover, pp. 1–31.

Joerstad, M. (2019). *The Hebrew Bible and Environmental Ethics: Humans, Non-Humans, and the Living Landscape*. Cambridge: Cambridge University Press.

Johnson, M. R. (2005). *Aristotle on Teleology*. Oxford: Oxford University Press.

Kaufman, G. D. (2001). On thinking of God as serendipitous creativity. *Journal of the American Academy of Religion* **69**(2), 409–25. http://doi:10.1093/jaarel/69.2.409.

Kauffman, S. A. (2008). *Reinventing the Sacred: A New View of Science, Reason, and Religion*. New York: Basic Books.

Kenny, A. (2009). Agnosticism and atheism. In J. Cornwell and M. McGhee, eds., *Philosophers and God: At the Frontiers of Faith and Reason*. London: Bloomsbury, pp. 117–24.

Kimmerer, R. W. (2013). *Braiding Sweetgrass: Indigenous Wisdom, Scientific Knowledge and the Teachings of Plants*. Harmondsworth: Penguin.

Kingsbury, J. (2022). Taking taniwha seriously. *Asian Journal of Philosophy* **1**(49), 1–15. http://doi:10.1007/s44204-022-00052-0.

Kitcher, P. (2018). Deweyian naturalism. In M. Baggar, ed., *Pragmatism and Naturalism: Scientific and Social Inquiry After Representationalism*. New York: Columbia University Press, pp. 66–88.

Knight, C. C. (2005). Divine action: A neo-Byzantine model. *International Journal for Philosophy of Religion* **58**(3), 181–99. http://doi:10.1007/s11153-005-1076-5.

Knight, C. C. (2007). Emergence, naturalism, and panentheism: An eastern Christian perspective. In P. Clayton, ed., *All That Is: A Naturalistic Faith for the Twenty-First Century*. Minneapolis, MN: Fortress Press, pp. 81–92.

Kraut, R. (2011). *Against Absolute Goodness*. Oxford: Oxford University Press.

Leidenhag, J. (2020). Deploying panpsychism for the demarcation of panentheism. In G. Brüntrup, B. P. Göcke, and L. Jaskolla, eds., *Panentheism and Panpsychism: Philosophy of Religion Meets Philosophy of Mind*. Leiden: Brill, pp. 65–90.

Leidenhag, J. (2021). *Minding Creation: Theological Panpsychism and the Doctrine of Creation*. London: Bloomsbury/T&T Clark.

Leidenhag, J. (2024). Minding creation: Response to critics. *Religious Studies* **60**(3), 497–506. http://doi:10.1017/S0034412523001038.

Leidenhag, M. (2021). *Naturalizing God? A Critical Evaluation of Religious Naturalism*. Albany, NY: State University of New York Press.

Leidenhag, M. (2024). Christianity and religious naturalism. In B. N. Wolfe et al., eds., *St Andrews Encyclopaedia of Theology*. www.saet.ac.uk/Christianity/ReligiousNaturalism.

Leopold, A. (1949). *A Sand County Almanac*. New York: Oxford University Press.

Leslie, J. (1979). *Value and Existence*. Totowa: Roman & Littlefield.

Levine, M. (1994). *Pantheism: A Non-theistic Concept of Deity*. London: Routledge.

Lewis, T. (1846) Has the state a religion? *The American (Whig) Review* **3**, 273–89.

Liu, J. (2014). Chinese qi-naturalism and liberal naturalism. *Philosophy, Theology and the Sciences* **1**(1), 59–86. http://doi:10.1628/219728314X13946985796952.

Lockhart, C., Houkamau, C. A., Sibley, C. G., and Osborne, D. (2019). To be at one with the land: Māori spirituality predicts greater environmental regard. *Religions* **10**(7), 427. http://doi:10.3390/rel10070427.

Macalister, T. (2021). Naturalistic religious practices: What naturalists have been discussing and doing. *Zygon* **56**(4), 1027–38. http://doi:10.1111/zygo.12744.

Macarthur, D. (2010). Taking the human sciences seriously. In M. De Caro and D. Macarthur, eds., *Naturalism and Normativity*. New York: Columbia University Press, pp. 123–41.

MacIntyre, A. (1967). Pantheism. In P. Edwards, ed., *The Encyclopedia of Philosophy*, Vol. 5. New York: Macmillan and the Free Press, pp. 31-35.

Marsden, M. (2003). *The Woven Universe: Selected Writings of Rev. Māori Marsden*. Edited by T. A. C. Royal. Otaki, NZ: The Estate of Rev Māori Marsden.

McFague, S. (1990). Imagining a theology of nature: The world as God's body. In C. Birch, W. Eaken, and J. B. McDaniel, eds., *Liberating Life: Contemporary Approaches in Ecological Theology*. Maryknoll, NY: Orbis Books, pp. 201–27.

McKirkland, C. and Fuimaono, E. (2024). Engaging with J. Leidenhag's *Minding Creation: Theological Panpsychism and the Doctrine of Creation*. *Religious Studies* **60**(3), 472–77. http://doi:10.1017/S0034412523000215.

Mesle, R. C. (1993). *Process Theology: A Basic Introduction*. St. Louis, MO: Chalice Press.

Mika, C. (2023). The problem of the spiritual thing. *Asian Journal of Philosophy* **2**(74), 1–6. http://doi:10.1007/s44204-023-00132-9.

Mulgan, T. (2015). *Purpose in the Universe: The Moral and Metaphysical Case for Ananthropocentric Purposivism*. Oxford: Oxford University Press.

Mulgan, T. (2022). Could we worship a non-human-centred impersonal cosmic purpose? In G. Gasser and S. Kittle, eds., *The Divine Nature: Personal and A-Personal Perspectives*. New York: Routledge, pp. 285–302.

Mullins, R. T. (2016). The difficulty with demarcating panentheism. *Sophia* **55**(3), 325–46. http://doi:10.1007/s11841-015-0497-6.

Nadler, S. (2023). Baruch Spinoza. In E. N. Zalta and U. Nodelman, eds., *The Stanford Encyclopedia of Philosophy* (Spring 2024 Edition) https://plato.stanford.edu/archives/spr2024/entries/spinoza/.

Nagel, Thomas (2012). *Mind and Cosmos: Why the Materialist Neo-Darwinian Conception of Nature Is Almost Certainly False*. New York: Oxford University Press.

Norton-Smith, T. (2018). One Shawnee's reflections on religious naturalism. In D. A. Crosby and J. A. Stone, eds., *The Routledge Handbook of Religious Naturalism*. New York: Routledge, pp. 218–29.

Nygren, A. (1932 and 1938/9). *Agape and Eros: Parts I & II*. Translated by P. S. Watson. Philadelphia: Westminster Press. (Part I was first published in 1932; Part II, Vol. I, was published in 1938; Part II, Vol. II, was published in 1939. The work was revised, in part retranslated and published in one volume in 1953.)

Oppy, G. (2018). *Naturalism and Religion: A Contemporary Philosophical Investigation*. New York: Routledge.

Ouis, S. P. (1998). Islamic ecotheology based on the Qur'an. *Islamic Studies* **37**(2), 151–81. https://www.jstor.org/stable/20836989.

Peacocke, A. (2007a). *All That Is: A Naturalistic Faith for the Twenty-First Century*. Edited by Philip Clayton. Minneapolis, MN: Fortress Press.

Peacocke, A. (2007b). A Naturalistic Christian Faith for the Twenty-First Century: An Essay in Interpretation. In *All That Is: A Naturalistic Faith for the Twenty-First Century*. Minneapolis, MN: Fortress Press, pp. 3–56.

Peters, K. E. (2002). *Dancing with the Sacred: Evolution, Ecology, and God*. Harrisburg, PA: Trinity Press International.

Peters, K. E. (2022). *Christian Naturalism: Christian Thinking for Living in This World Only*. Eugene, OR: Wipf & Stock.

Pizza, M. and Lewis, J., eds. (2009). *Handbook of Contemporary Paganism*. Leiden: E. J. Brill.

Pfeifer, K. (2020). Naïve panentheism. In G. Brüntrup, B. P. Göcke, and L. Jaskolla, eds., *Panentheism and Panpsychism: Philosophy of Religion Meets Philosophy of Mind*. Leiden: Brill, pp. 123–38.

Plantinga, A. (2011). *Where the Conflict Really Lies: Science, Religion, and Naturalism*. New York: Oxford University Press.

Plato. Euthyphro. In E. Hamilton and H. Cairns, eds., *The Collected Dialogues of Plato: Including the Letters*. Princeton: Princeton University Press, 1961, pp. 169–85.

Psillos, S. (1999). *Scientific Realism: How Science Tracks Truth*. London: Routledge.

Rescher, N. (1984). *The Riddle of Existence: An Essay in Idealistic Metaphysics*. New York: University Press of America.

Roberts, M. (2012). Revisiting 'the natural world of the Māori'. In D. Keenan, ed., *Huia Histories of Māori*. Wellington: Huia Press, pp. 33–56.

Rue, L. D. (2004). *Religion Is Not about God: How Spiritual Traditions Nurture Our Biological Nature and What to Expect When They Fail*. New Brunswick, NJ: Rutgers University Press.

Rue, L. D. (2011). *Nature is Enough: Religious Naturalism and the Meaning of Life*. Albany, NY: State University of New York Press.

Russell, G. K. (2023), *Barriers to Entailment: Hume's Law and other Limits on Logical Consequence*. Oxford: Oxford University Press.

Schellenberg, J. L. (2013). *Evolutionary Religion*. Oxford: Oxford University Press.

Schellenberg, J. L. (2016). God for all time: From theism to ultimism. In A. Buchareff and Y. Nagasawa, eds., *Alternative Concepts of God: Essays on the Metaphysics of the Divine*. Oxford: Oxford University Press, pp. 164–77.

Skrbina, D. (2017). Panpsychism in the West (revised edition). Cambridge, MA: MIT Press.

Sorrell, R. D. (2009). *St Francis of Assisi and Nature: Tradition and Innovation in Western Christian Attitudes toward the Environment*. New York: Oxford University Press.

Speaks, J. B. (2024). Transcendence, immanence, and ultimacy: The theological adequacy of religious naturalism. *American Journal of Theology & Philosophy* **45**(2), 44–59. https://jhu.edu/article/943318.

Spencer, A. J. (2019). The modernistic roots of our ecological crisis: The Lynn White thesis at fifty. *Journal of Markets & Morality* **22**(2), 355–71.

www.proquest.com/scholarly-journals/modernistic-roots-our-ecological-crisis-lynn/docview/2510296013/se-2.

Spinoza, B. (2005 [1677]). *Ethics*. Translated by E. M.Curley, with an introduction by S. Hampshire. London: Penguin Classics.

Starhawk (1999). *The Spiral Dance, 20th Anniversary: A Rebirth of the Ancient Religion of the Great Goddess*. San Francisco: HarperOne.

Steinhart, E. (2017). Religion after naturalism. In P. Draper and J. L. Schellenberg, eds., *Renewing Philosophy of Religion: Exploratory Essays*. Oxford: Oxford University Press, pp. 63–78.

Steinhart, E. (2018). Practices in religious naturalism. In J. A. Stone and D. A. Crosby, eds., *The Routledge Handbook of Religious Naturalism*. London: Routledge, pp. 341–51.

Steinhart E. (2023). *Atheistic Platonism: A manifesto*. Cham, Switzerland: Palgrave Macmillan.

Steinhart, E. (2025a). *Contemporary Pagan Philosophy*. Cambridge: Cambridge University Press. http://doi:10.1017/9781009452373.

Steinhart, E (2025b). Pagan religious naturalism. *Neue Zeitschrift für Systematische Theologie und Religionsphilosophie* **67**(2), 162–68. https://doi.org/10.1515/nzsth-2025-0004.

Stenmark, M. (2013). Religious naturalism and its rivals. *Religious Studies* **49**(4), 529–50. http://doi:10.1017/S0034412512000431.

Stone, J. A. (2003). Varieties of religious naturalism. *Zygon* **38**(1), 89–93. http://doi:10.1111/1467-9744.00480.

Stone, J. A. (2008). *Religious Naturalism Today: The Rebirth of a Forgotten Alternative*. Albany, NY: State University of New York Press.

Stone, J. A. (2017). *Sacred Nature: The Environmental Potential of Religious Naturalism*. New York: Routledge.

Stone, J. A. (2018). Defining and defending religious naturalism. In D. A. Crosby and J. A. Stone, eds., *The Routledge Handbook of Religious Naturalism*. London: Routledge, pp. 7–18.

Tassell-Matamua, N., Lindsay, N., Moriarty, T. R., and Haami, D. (2021). Indigenous Māori notions of spirit and spirituality as enablers of resilience and flourishing in Aotearoa New Zealand. In H. N. Weaver, ed., *The Routledge International Handbook of Indigenous Resilience*. London: Rouledge, pp. 81–95.

Tassell-Matamua, N., MacDonald-Nepe, K., Moriarty, T. R., and Tahuri, T. (2023). Indigenous Māori notions of consciousness, soul, and spirit. *Journal of Consciousness Studies* **30**(5), 151–65. http://doi:10.53765/20512201.30.5.151.

Teilhard de Chardin, P. (1999 [1955]). *The Human Phenomenon*. Edited and translated by S. Appleton-Weber. Brighton: Sussex Academic Press.

Thompson, M. (2008). *Life and Action: Elementary Structures of Practice and Practical Thought*. Cambridge, MA: Harvard University Press.

Tillich, P. (1957). *Systematic Theology*, Vol. II. *Existence and the Christ*. Chicago: University of Chicago Press.

Tugby, M. (2024). *Teleology*. Cambridge: Cambridge University Press.

van Roojen, M. (2023). Moral cognitivism vs. non-cognitivism. In E. N. Zalta and U. Nodelman, eds., *The Stanford Encyclopedia of Philosophy* (Summer 2024 Edition). https://plato.stanford.edu/archives/sum2024/entries/moral-cognitivism/.

Viney, D. (2022). Process theism. In E. N. Zalta, ed., *The Stanford Encyclopedia of Philosophy* (Summer 2022 Edition). https://plato.stanford.edu/archives/sum2022/entries/process-theism/.

Watene, K. (2023). Taniwha, taonga, and tangata. *Asian Journal of Philosophy* **2**(56), 1–7. http://doi:10.1007/s44204-023-00112-z.

Wheeler, D. (2018). Deus sive Natura: Pantheism as a variety of religious naturalism. In D. A. Crosby and J. A. Stone, eds., *The Routledge Handbook of Religious Naturalism*. New York: Routledge, pp. 106–17.

White, L. (1967). Historical roots of our ecological crisis. *Science* **155**(3767), 1203-1207. http://doi:10.1126/science.155.3767.1203.

Wieman, H. N. (1946). *The Source of Human Good*. Chicago: University of Chicago Press.

Wildman, W. J. (2006). 'Ground-of-Being Theologies', in P. Clayton and Z. Simpson, eds., *The Oxford Handbook of Religion and Science*. Oxford: Oxford University Press, pp. 612–32. http://doi:10.1093/oxfordhb/9780199543656.001.0001.

Wittgenstein, L. (1961 [1922]). *Tractatus Logico-Philosophicus*. Translated by D.F. Pears and B.F.McGuiness. London: Routledge and Kegan Paul.

Yao, X. (1996). *Confucianism and Christianity: A Comparative Study of Jen and Agape*. Brighton: Sussex Academic.

Acknowledgments

We wish to thank Yujin Nagasawa for inviting us to write this Element and for his feedback on a precursor of it. This Element grew out of the 2024 Munich Lecture in Philosophy of Religion, which we delivered at Ludwig Maximilian University on 14 May. Our thanks to Sebastian Gäb for inviting us to give that lecture, and to Thomas Schärtl-Trendel for making our extended visit to Munich possible. A slightly expanded published version of the Munich Lecture (under the title 'Varieties of Religious Naturalism: A Conceptual Investigation') has been published in *Neue Zeitschrift für Systematische Theologie und Religionsphilosophie*, along with discussion from three commentators and our reply. During our work on this project, we had useful conversations with and feedback from many people, including audiences at our Munich lecture and seminars at the University of Auckland, the University of Waikato, and the 2024 annual conference of the New Zealand Association of Philosophy at the University of Otago. We are grateful to two anonymous reviewers for Cambridge University Press for helpful comments on previous drafts.

Thompson, M. (2008). *Life and Action: Elementary Structures of Practice and Practical Thought*. Cambridge, MA: Harvard University Press.

Tillich, P. (1957). *Systematic Theology*, Vol. II. *Existence and the Christ*. Chicago: University of Chicago Press.

Tugby, M. (2024). *Teleology*. Cambridge: Cambridge University Press.

van Roojen, M. (2023). Moral cognitivism vs. non-cognitivism. In E. N. Zalta and U. Nodelman, eds., *The Stanford Encyclopedia of Philosophy* (Summer 2024 Edition). https://plato.stanford.edu/archives/sum2024/entries/moral-cognitivism/.

Viney, D. (2022). Process theism. In E. N. Zalta, ed., *The Stanford Encyclopedia of Philosophy* (Summer 2022 Edition). https://plato.stanford.edu/archives/sum2022/entries/process-theism/.

Watene, K. (2023). Taniwha, taonga, and tangata. *Asian Journal of Philosophy* **2**(56), 1–7. http://doi:10.1007/s44204-023-00112-z.

Wheeler, D. (2018). Deus sive Natura: Pantheism as a variety of religious naturalism. In D. A. Crosby and J. A. Stone, eds., *The Routledge Handbook of Religious Naturalism*. New York: Routledge, pp. 106–17.

White, L. (1967). Historical roots of our ecological crisis. *Science* **155**(3767), 1203-1207. http://doi:10.1126/science.155.3767.1203.

Wieman, H. N. (1946). *The Source of Human Good*. Chicago: University of Chicago Press.

Wildman, W. J. (2006). 'Ground-of-Being Theologies', in P. Clayton and Z. Simpson, eds., *The Oxford Handbook of Religion and Science*. Oxford: Oxford University Press, pp. 612–32. http://doi:10.1093/oxfordhb/9780199543656.001.0001.

Wittgenstein, L. (1961 [1922]). *Tractatus Logico-Philosophicus*. Translated by D.F. Pears and B.F.McGuiness. London: Routledge and Kegan Paul.

Yao, X. (1996). *Confucianism and Christianity: A Comparative Study of Jen and Agape*. Brighton: Sussex Academic.

Acknowledgments

We wish to thank Yujin Nagasawa for inviting us to write this Element and for his feedback on a precursor of it. This Element grew out of the 2024 Munich Lecture in Philosophy of Religion, which we delivered at Ludwig Maximilian University on 14 May. Our thanks to Sebastian Gäb for inviting us to give that lecture, and to Thomas Schärtl-Trendel for making our extended visit to Munich possible. A slightly expanded published version of the Munich Lecture (under the title 'Varieties of Religious Naturalism: A Conceptual Investigation') has been published in *Neue Zeitschrift für Systematische Theologie und Religionsphilosophie*, along with discussion from three commentators and our reply. During our work on this project, we had useful conversations with and feedback from many people, including audiences at our Munich lecture and seminars at the University of Auckland, the University of Waikato, and the 2024 annual conference of the New Zealand Association of Philosophy at the University of Otago. We are grateful to two anonymous reviewers for Cambridge University Press for helpful comments on previous drafts.

Cambridge Elements ≡

Global Philosophy of Religion

Yujin Nagasawa
University of Oklahoma

Yujin Nagasawa is Kingfisher College Chair of the Philosophy of Religion and Ethics and Professor of Philosophy at the University of Oklahoma. He is the author of *The Problem of Evil for Atheists* (2024), *Maximal God: A New Defence of Perfect Being Theism* (2018), *Miracles: A Very Short Introduction* (2018), *The Existence of God: A Philosophical Introduction* (2011), and *God and Phenomenal Consciousness* (2008), along with numerous articles. He is the editor-in-chief of *Religious Studies* and served as the president of the British Society for the Philosophy of Religion from 2017 to 2019.

About the Series

This Cambridge Elements series provides concise and structured overviews of a wide range of religious beliefs and practices, with an emphasis on global, multi-faith viewpoints. Leading scholars from diverse cultural backgrounds and geographical regions explore topics and issues that have been overlooked by Western philosophy of religion.

Cambridge Elements⁼

Global Philosophy of Religion

Elements in the Series

Afro-Brazilian Religions
José Eduardo Porcher

The African Mood Perspective on God and the Problem of Evil
Ada Agada

Contemporary Pagan Philosophy
Eric Steinhart

Semi-Secular Worldviews and the Belief in Something Beyond
Carl-Johan Palmqvist, Francis Jonbäck

Zoroastrianism and Contemporary Philosophy
Daniel Nolan

Karma and Rebirth in Hinduism
Swami Medhananda

Religious Naturalism
John Bishop and Ken Perszyk

A full series listing is available at: www.cambridge.org/EGPR

For EU product safety concerns, contact us at Calle de José Abascal, 56–1°,
28003 Madrid, Spain or eugpsr@cambridge.org.

www.ingramcontent.com/pod-product-compliance
Lightning Source LLC
LaVergne TN
LVHW011856060526
838200LV00054B/4362